Advisory Editor

Edwin S. Gaustad

CHURCH AND STATE

IN

THE UNITED STATES

OR

THE AMERICAN IDEA OF RELIGIOUS LIBERTY AND ITS PRACTICAL EFFECTS

BY

PHILIP SCHAFF, D.D., LL.D.

ARNO PRESS

A NEW YORK TIMES COMPANY

New York • 1972

Reprint Edition 1972 by Arno Press Inc.

Reprinted from a copy in
The State Historical Society of Wisconsin Library

RELIGION IN AMERICA - Series II
ISBN for complete set: 0-405-04050-4
See last pages of this volume for titles.

Manufactured in the United States of America

Publisher's Note: Reprinted from PAPERS OF THE
AMERICAN HISTORICAL ASSOCIATION, Vol.II, No.4,
New York and London, 1888. BR
516
.S3
1972

Library of Congress Cataloging in Publication Data

Schaff, Philip, 1819-1893.
    Church and state in the United States.

    (Religion in America, series II)
    Original ed. issued as vol. 2, no. 4 of the Papers of
the American Historical Association series.
    1. Church and state in the United States.
2. Religious liberty--U. S. I. Series: American
Historical Association. Papers, v. 2, no. 4.
BR516.S3 1972   261.7'0973   75-38462
ISBN 0-405-04083-0

PAPERS

OF THE

AMERICAN
HISTORICAL ASSOCIATION

VOL. II.   NO. 4

CHURCH AND STATE

IN

THE UNITED STATES

OR

THE AMERICAN IDEA OF RELIGIOUS LIBERTY AND ITS PRACTICAL EFFECTS

WITH OFFICIAL DOCUMENTS

BY

PHILIP SCHAFF, D.D., LL.D.

PROFESSOR OF CHURCH HISTORY IN THE UNION THEOLOGICAL SEMINARY AT NEW YORK

NEW YORK & LONDON

G. P. PUTNAM'S SONS

The Knickerbocker Press

1888

Press of

G. P. PUTNAM'S SONS

New York

PREFACE.

This little work is a contribution to American Church History, and to the Centennial Celebration of our National Constitution. It discusses that part of the Constitution which protects us against the despotism of a state church, and guarantees to us the free exercise and enjoyment of religion, as an inherent, inviolable, and inalienable right of every man. The First Amendment is the *Magna Charta* of that freedom, and well worthy to be set forth in its true light with its antecedents, surroundings, and effects at home and abroad. This I have endeavored to do, for the first time, from the stand-point of a church historian and theologian.

American Church History has yet to be written. We are so busy making history that we have little time to study and to write history. But monographs on sectional and local topics are multiplying fast, and already present a formidable mass of material for a comprehensive view of the whole field.

There is scarcely a more inviting task for a rising American historian than to exhibit from the broad platform of truth and justice, in life-like reproduction, the genesis and growth of American Christianity in its connections with the mother Christianity of Europe, its distinctive peculiarities, and its great mission for the future.

THE AUTHOR.

Union Theological Seminary, New York,
Nov. 24, 1887.

CONTENTS.

Official Documents and Standard Opinions on Religious Liberty.

CHURCH AND STATE IN THE UNITED STATES.

What is the distinctive character of American Christianity in its organized social aspect and its relation to the national life, as compared with the Christianity of Europe?

It is a FREE CHURCH IN A FREE STATE, or a SELF-SUP- PORTING AND SELF-GOVERNING CHRISTIANITY IN INDEPEND- ENT BUT FRIENDLY RELATION TO THE CIVIL GOVERNMENT.

This relationship of church and state marks an epoch. It is a new chapter in the history of Christianity, and the most important one which America has so far contributed. It lies at the base of our religious institutions and opera- tions, and they cannot be understood without it. And yet, strange to say, it has never received the treatment it de- serves, either from the historical or the philosophical point of view, although it is often incidentally mentioned, espe- cially in discussions of religion in the public schools. It seems to be regarded as a self-evident fact and truth which need no explanation and defence. I know of no ecclesiasti- cal or secular history, or special treatise, which gives a satis- factory account of it ; and the works on the Constitution of the United States touch only on the legal aspect of the religious clauses, or pass them by altogether.

THE AMERICAN THEORY.

The relationship of church and state in the United States secures full liberty of religious thought, speech, and action, within the limits of the public peace and order. It makes persecution impossible.

Religion and liberty are inseparable. Religion is volun- tary, and cannot, and ought not to be forced.

This is a fundamental article of the American creed, without distinction of sect or party. Liberty, both civil and religious, is an American instinct. All natives suck it in with
the mother's milk; all immigrants accept it as a happy
boon, especially those who flee from oppression and persecution abroad. Even those who reject the modern theory
of liberty enjoy the practice, and would defend it in their
own interest against any attempt to overthrow it.

Such liberty is impossible on the basis of a union of
church and state, where the one of necessity restricts or
controls the other. It requires a friendly separation, where
each power is entirely independent in its own sphere. The
church, as such, has nothing to do with the state except to
obey its laws and to strengthen its moral foundations; the
state has nothing to do with the church except to protect
her in her property and liberty; and the state must be
equally just to all forms of belief and unbelief which do not
endanger the public safety.

The family, the church, and the state are divine institutions demanding alike our obedience, in their proper sphere
of jurisdiction. The family is the oldest institution, and
the source of church and state. The patriarchs were priests
and kings of their households. Church and state are equally
necessary, and as inseparable as soul and body, and yet as
distinct as soul and body. The church is instituted for the
religious interests and eternal welfare of man; the state
for his secular interests and temporal welfare. The one
looks to heaven as the final home of immortal spirits, the
other upon our mother earth. The church is the reign of
love; the state is the reign of justice. The former is
governed by the gospel, the latter by the law. The church
exhorts, and uses moral suasion; the state commands, and
enforces obedience. The church punishes by rebuke, sus-
pension, and excommunication; the state by fines, imprisonment, and death. Both meet on questions of public
morals, and both together constitute civilized human
society and ensure its prosperity.

The root of this theory we find in the New Testament.

In the ancient world religion and politics were blended. Among the Jews religion ruled the state, which was a theocracy. Among the heathen the state ruled religion; the Roman emperor was the supreme pontiff (*pontifex maximus*), the gods were national, and the priests were servants of the state.

Christianity had at first no official connection with the state.

Christ directs us to render unto God the things that are God's, and unto Cæsar the things that are Cæsar's (Matt. xxii., 21). He paid the tribute money to the Jewish temple and obeyed the laws of Rome, but he refused to be a judge and divider of the inheritance of two brothers, as lying outside of the sphere of religion (Luke xii., 14). He declared before Pilate that his kingdon is not of this world (John xviii., 36), and rebuked Peter for drawing the sword, even in defence of his Master (John xviii., 11). When the Evil One tempted him with the possession of all the kingdoms of this world, he said unto him : "Get thee hence, Satan " (Matt. iv., 10). Secular power has proved a satanic gift to the church, and ecclesiastical power has proved an engine of tyranny in the hands of the state.[1] The apostles used only the spiritual weapons of truth and love in spreading the gospel of salvation. They enjoined obedience to the civil power, even under Nero (Rom. xiii., 1 : 7), but they would rather suffer imprisonment and death than obey even their own Jewish magistrate against the dictates of their conscience (Acts iv., 29).

If men had always acted on this principle and example, history would have been spared the horrors of persecution and religious wars.

For three hundred years the Christian church kept aloof from politics, and, while obeying the civil laws and paying

---

[1] The well-known lines of Dante (" Inferno," xix., 113-118) which refer to the fictitious donation of Constantine the Great, may be quoted here with a wider application :

> " Ah, Constantine! of how much ill was mother,
> Not thy conversion, but that marriage-dower
> Which the first wealthy Pope received of thee."

tribute, maintained at the same time the higher law of conscience in refusing to comply with idolatrous customs and in professing the faith in the face of death. The early Apologists—Justin Martyr, Tertullian, Lactantius—boldly claimed the freedom of religion as a natural right.[1] When the first blood of heretics (the Priscillianists in Spain) was shed, in 385, the better feeling of the church, as expressed by Ambrose of Milan, and Martin of Tours, shrank from it in horror.[2]

THE AMERICAN SYSTEM COMPARED WITH OTHER SYSTEMS.

The American relationship of church and state differs from all previous relationships in Europe and in the colonial period of our history ; and yet it rests upon them and reaps the benefit of them all. For history is an organic unit, and American history has its roots in Europe.

1. The American system differs from the ante-Nicene or pre-Constantinian separation of church and state, when the church was indeed, as with us, self-supporting and self-governing, and so far free within, but under persecution from without, being treated as a forbidden religion by the then heathen state. In America the government protects the church in her property and rights without interfering with her internal affairs. By the power of truth and the moral heroism of martyrdom the church converted the Roman Empire and became the mother of Christian states.

2. The American system differs from the hierarchical control of the church over the state, or from priest government, which prevailed in the Middle Ages down to the Reformation, and reached its culmination in the Papacy. It confines the church to her proper spiritual vocation, and leaves the state independent in all the temporal affairs of the nation. The hierarchical theory was suited to the times after the fall of the Roman Empire and the ancient civilization, when the state was a rude military despotism, when the church was

---

[1] Schaff, "Church History" (revised ed.), II. 35 *sq.*
[2] *Ibid.*, vol. III. 143.

the refuge of the people, when the Christian priesthood was in sole possession of learning and had to civilize as well as to evangelize the barbarians of northern and western Europe. By her influence over legislation the church abolished bad laws and customs, introduced benevolent institutions, and created a Christian state controlled by the spirit of justice and humanity, and fit for self-government.

3. The American system differs from the Erastian or Cæsaro-Papal control of the state over the church, which obtained in the old Byzantine Empire, and prevails in modern Russia, and in the Protestant states of Europe, where the civil government protects and supports the church, but at the expense of her dignity and independence, and deprives her of the power of self-government. The Erastian system was based on the assumption that all citizens are also Christians of one creed, but is abnormal in the mixed character of government and people in the modern state. In America, the state has no right whatever to interfere with the affairs of the church, her doctrine, discipline, and worship, and the appointment of ministers. It would be a great calamity if religion were to become subject to our ever-changing politics.

4. The American system differs from the system of toleration, which began in Germany with the Westphalia Treaty, 1648; in England with the Act of Toleration, 1689, and which now prevails over nearly all Europe; of late years, nominally at least, even in Roman Catholic countries, to the very gates of the Vatican, in spite of the protest of the Pope. Toleration exists where the government supports one or more churches, and permits other religious communities under the name of sects (as on the continent), or dissenters and nonconformists (as in England), under certain conditions. In America, there are no such distinctions, but only churches or denominations on a footing of perfect equality before the law. To talk about any particular denomination as *the* church, or *the American* church, has no meaning, and betrays ignorance or conceit. Such exclusiveness is natural and logical in Romanism, but unnatural, illogical, and contemptible in any other church. The American laws know no such institution

as " the church," but only separate and independent organizations.

Toleration is an important step from state-churchism to free-churchism.   But it is only a step.   There is a very great difference between toleration and liberty.   Toleration is a concession, which may be withdrawn ; it implies a preference for the ruling form of faith and worship, and a practical disapproval of all other forms.   It may be coupled with many restrictions and disabilities.   We tolerate what we dislike, but cannot alter; we tolerate even a nuisance if we must.   Acts of toleration are wrung from a government by the force of circumstances and the power of a minority too influential to be disregarded.   In this way even the most despotic governments, as those of Turkey and of Russia, are tolerant ; the one toward Christians and Jews, the other toward Mohammedans and dissenters from the orthodox Greek Church ; but both deny the right of self-extension and missionary operations except in favor of the state religion, and both forbid and punish apostasy from it.   Prince Gortschakoff, the late chancellor of the Russian Empire, before an international deputation of the Evangelical Alliance, pleading for religious freedom in behalf of the persecuted Lutherans of the Baltic provinces in 1871, boldly declared, within my hearing, that Russia was the most tolerant country in the world, and pointed in proof to half a dozen churches of different denominations in the principal street of St. Petersburg, but protested at the same time against what he called propagandism.   The great Russian statesman did not, or would not understand the vast difference between toleration and liberty.   The English Lord Stanhope, in a speech in the House of Lords in 1827, on the Bill for the Repeal of the Test and Corporation Acts, said: "The time was, when toleration was craved by dissenters as a boon ; it is now demanded as a right ; but a time will come when it will be spurned as an insult."

In our country we ask no toleration for religion and its free exercise, but we claim it as an inalienable right.   " It is not toleration," says Judge Cooley, " which is established in

our system, but religious equality." Freedom of religion is
one of the greatest gifts of God to man, without distinction
of race and color. He is the author and lord of conscience,
and no power on earth has a right to stand between God and
the conscience. A violation of this divine law written in
the heart is an assault upon the majesty of God and the
image of God in man. Granting the freedom of conscience,
we must, by logical necessity, also grant the freedom of its
manifestation and exercise in public worship. To concede
the first and to deny the second, after the manner of despotic
governments, is to imprison the conscience. To be just, the
state must either support all or none of the religions of its
citizens. Our government supports none, but protects all.

5. Finally—and this we would emphasize as especially important in our time,—the American system differs radically
and fundamentally from the infidel and red-republican theory
of religious freedom. The word freedom is one of the most
abused words in the vocabulary. True liberty is a positive
force, regulated by law ; false liberty is a negative force, a
release from restraint. True liberty is the moral power of
self-government; the liberty of infidels and anarchists is
carnal licentiousness. The American separation of church
and state rests on respect for the church ; the infidel separation, on indifference and hatred of the church, and of religion
itself.

The infidel theory was tried and failed in the first Revolution of France. It began with toleration, and ended with
the abolition of Christianity, and with the reign of terror,
which in turn prepared the way for military despotism as
the only means of saving society from anarchy and ruin.
Our infidels and anarchists would re-enact this tragedy if
they should ever get the power. They openly profess their
hatred and contempt of our Sunday-laws, our Sabbaths, our
churches, and all our religious institutions and societies. Let
us beware of them ! The American system grants freedom
also to irreligion and infidelity, but only within the limits of
the order and safety of society. The destruction of religion
would be the destruction of morality and the ruin of the

state. Civil liberty requires for its support religious liberty, and cannot prosper without it. Religious liberty is not an empty sound, but an orderly exercise of religious duties and enjoyment of all its privileges. It is freedom *in* religion, not freedom *from* religion ; as true civil liberty is freedom *in* law, and not freedom *from* law. Says Goethe :

> " *In der Beschränkung erst zeigt sich der Meister,*
> *Und das Gesetz nur kann dir Freiheit geben.*"

Republican institutions in the hands of a virtuous and God-fearing nation are the very best in the world, but in the hands of a corrupt and irreligious people they are the very worst, and the most effective weapons of destruction. An indignant people may rise in rebellion against a cruel tyrant ; but who will rise against the tyranny of the people in possession of the ballot-box and the whole machinery of government ? Here lies our great danger, and it is increasing every year.

Destroy our churches, close our Sunday-schools, abolish the Lord's Day, and our republic would become an empty shell, and our people would tend to heathenism and barbarism. Christianity is the most powerful factor in our society and the pillar of our institutions. It regulates the family ; it enjoins private and public virtue ; it builds up moral character ; it teaches us to love God supremely, and our neighbor as ourselves ; it makes good men and useful citizens ; it denounces every vice ; it encourages every virtue ; it promotes and serves the public welfare ; it upholds peace and order. Christianity is the only possible religion for the American people, and with Christianity are bound up all our hopes for the future.

This was strongly felt by Washington, the father of his country, " first in war, first in peace, and first in the hearts of his countrymen " ; and no passage in his immortal farewell address is more truthful, wise, and worthy of constant remembrance by every American statesman and citizen than that in which he affirms the inseparable connection of religion with morality and national prosperity.

THE CONSTITUTIONAL BASIS OF THE AMERICAN SYSTEM.

The legal basis of American Christianity in its relation to the civil government is laid down in the Constitution of the United States, which this year enters upon its second centennial.

This great document was framed after the achievement of national independence in a convention of delegates from twelve of the original States (all except Rhode Island), in the city of Philadelphia, between May 14th and September 17, 1787, by the combined wisdom of such statesmen as Hamilton, Madison, King, Morris, Sherman, Dickinson, Pinckney, Franklin, under the presiding genius of Washington. It was ratified by eleven States before the close of the year 1788, and went into operation in March, 1789.[1] It was materially improved by ten amendments, which were recommended by several States as a guarantee of fundamental rights, proposed by the first Congress in 1789–90, and adopted in 1791. To these were subsequently added five new amendments, namely: Article XI. in 1793; Article XII. in 1803; Article XIII. in 1865; Article XIV. in 1868; Article XV. in 1870. The last three are the result of the civil war, and forbid slavery, declare the citizenship of all persons born or naturalized in the United States, and secure the right of citizens to vote irrespective " of race, color, or previous condition of servitude."

[1] Delaware (Dec. 7, 1787), New Jersey (Dec. 18, 1787), Georgia (Jan. 2, 1788), and Maryland (April 28, 1788) ratified the Constitution unanimously and unconditionally ; Pennsylvania (Dec. 12, 1787), with a majority of 15 (45 out of 60) ; Connecticut (Jan. 9, 1788), with a majority of 88 (128 against 40) ; Massachusetts (Feb. 7, 1788), by a vote of 187 to 168 ; South Carolina (May 23, 1788), with three recommendations ; Virginia (July 26, 1788), by a majority of 10 (89 to 79), and with a declaration of a bill of rights ; New Hampshire (June 21, 1788), with twelve alterations and provisions ; New York (July 26, 1788), with a majority of only three (30 to 27). The remaining two States adopted the Constitution afterward—North Carolina, November 21, 1789 ; Rhode Island, May 29, 1790. During the deliberations for its adoption, it was ably defended by Alexander Hamilton, of New York, James Madison, of Virginia, and John Jay, of New York, in *The Federalist* (1787 to 1788), against the attacks of the anti-Federalists—newly edited by John C. Hamilton, Philadelphia (Lippincott & Co.), 1873, (659 pages). Another edition by Henry B. Dawson, New York, 1878 (615 pages). But *The Federalist* is silent on the subject of religion.

This Constitution, including the fifteen amendments, is "the supreme law of the land,"—that is, of all the States and Territories belonging to the United States. It expresses the sovereign will and authority of the people, which, under God, is the source of civil power and legislation in a free country. It can only be altered and amended by the same authority. Experience has proved its wisdom and deepened the attachment to its provisions. And, having stood the fiery ordeal of a gigantic civil war, it may be considered safe and sound for generations to come. Although by no means perfect, it is the best that could be made for this western republic by its thirty-nine framers, whom Alexander Hamilton Stephens (the Vice-President of the late Southern Confederacy) calls " the ablest body of jurists, legislators, and statesmen that has ever assembled on the continent of America." [1]   Most of them were conspicuous for practical experience in statesmanship and for services to the cause of liberty ; and they had the great advantage of drawing lessons of wisdom from the various State Constitutions, the Articles of Confederation, the British Constitution, the Swiss and Dutch Confederacies, as well as from ancient Greece and Rome. Their patriotism had been tried in the furnace of the War of Independence. James Madison, afterwards President of the United States, who preserved for posterity the debates of the Convention, gives it as his profound conviction, " that there never was an assembly of men, charged with a great and arduous trust, who were more pure in their motives, or more exclusively or anxiously devoted to the object committed to them, than were the members of the Federal Convention of 1787, to the object of devising and proposing a constitutional system which should best supply the defects of that which it was to replace, and best secure the permanent liberty and happiness of their country." [2]

[1] In Johnson's " Universal Cyclop.," revised edition, II. 243.

[2] In Jonathan Elliot's " Debates of the Several State Conventions on the Adoption of the Constitution," vol. V., p. 122. This and the following quotations are from the second and enlarged edition of this important work, published by Lippincott, Philadelphia, 1876, in 5 vols. The first edition, in 4 vols.,

The sessions were secret. The difficulties were serious: jealousies between the larger and smaller, the Northern and Southern States; differences of opinioncon cerning the continuation or prohibition of the African slave-trade ; the nature and extent of the executive, legislative, and judicial departments of the general government; and especially the power of the United States in relation to the separate States. At times, conciliation of the conflicting interests seemed hopeless, and it was during one of those periods of gloom that Dr. Franklin, then eighty-one years of age, read his remarkable speech in advocacy of seeking wisdom from the Almighty hearer of prayer.

But after four months of patient deliberation and mutual concession, the Constitution was matured and duly signed by all the delegates. It was by no means entirely new, but borrowed wisdom from the experience of the past as laid down in British and American documents of tried statesmanship and legislation ; and it is all the better for it. With this qualification we may accept the eulogy of W. E. Gladstone, one of the most learned of English statesmen, who calls the American Constitution " the most wonderful work ever struck off at a given time by the brain and purpose of man." [1] Cardinal Gibbons, of Baltimore, in accepting the invitation to attend the centennial celebration of the Constitution at Philadelphia, September, 1887, says : " The Constitution of the United States is worthy of being written in

---

appeared in Washington, 1830. The fifth volume contains Madison's diary of the debates in the Federal Convention, of which he was the most regular attendant and one of the most influential members. " The Madison Papers," purchased by order of Congress after his death, in his eighty-fifth year (June 28, 1836), were first published by Henry D. Gilpin, Washington, 1840, in 3 vols. The Debates of the Federal Convention are contained in vols. II. and III., and the passage quoted above is in vol. II., p. 718 *sq.*, at the close of his introduction to the Debates.

[1] Or, as he more recently expressed it : " The most remarkable work known to the modern times to have been produced by human intellect at a single stroke, so to speak, in its application to political affairs." See his letter of July 20, 1887, declining, for good reasons, a most flattering invitation to attend the centennial celebration of the Constitution, as the guest of the American people. And yet Gladstone doubted the success of the Union in the civil war.

letters of gold. It is a charter by which the liberties of sixty millions of people are secured, and by which, under Providence, the temporal happiness of countless millions yet unborn will be perpetuated." [1]   Justice Miller, in his memorial oration (September 17, 1887), finds the chief characteristic of the Constitution in this :   That " it is the first successful attempt in the history of the world to lay the deep and broad foundations of a government for millions of people and an unlimited territory in a single written instrument, framed and adopted in one great national effort.   This instrument comes nearer than any of political origin to Rousseau's idea of a society founded on a social contract.   In its formation, States and individuals, in the possession of equal rights—the rights of human nature common to all,—met together and deliberately agreed to give up certain of those rights to government for the better security of others ; and that there might be no mistake about this agreement it was reduced to writing, with all the solemnities which give sanction to the pledges of mankind."

ABOLITION OF RELIGIOUS TESTS.

Two provisions in this Constitution bear on the question of religion, and secure its freedom and independence.

1. The Constitution declares, in Article VI., § 3, that all senators and representatives of the United States, and the members of the several State legislatures, and all executive and judicial officers, both of the United States and of the several States, " shall be bound, by oath or affirmation, to support this Constitution : *but no religious test shall ever be required as a qualification to any office or public trust under the United States.*" [2]

This is negative, and excludes the establishment of any particular church or denomination as the national religion.

---

[1] Cardinal Gibbons made the concluding, Bishop Potter, of New York, the opening prayer at the celebration of September 17, 1887.

[2] I give the text and punctuation as in the original copy in the Department of State at Washington.   Elliot's " Debates," I. 5.

It secures the freedom and independence of the State from ecclesiastical domination and interference.

The clause was proposed by Charles Pinckney, of South Carolina. Roger Sherman "thought it unnecessary, the prevailing liberality being a sufficient security against such tests." Gouverneur Morris of Pennsylvania, and General Charles Cotesworth Pinckney of South Carolina approved the motion, whereupon "the motion was agreed to, *nem. con.*, and then the whole article. North Carolina only, no ; and Maryland divided."[1] The clause, however, as we shall see, met with considerable objection afterwards in Massachusetts and North Carolina.

Religious tests, whether of dogma or worship, were used by despotic governments, especially in England under the Stuarts, as means of excluding certain classes of persons, otherwise qualified, from public offices and their emoluments. Blackstone defends such tests as means of self-preservation, but is opposed to prosecution.[2] They were enforced in all American colonies, except in Rhode Island. The early settlers came from Europe to seek freedom for themselves, and then inconsistently denied it to others, from fear of losing the monopoly. In Massachusetts, Congregationalists had exclusive control; in Virginia the Church of England, for a century and a half. Even in the Quaker colony of Pennsylvania toleration was limited by the Toleration Act of 1689, contrary to the design of William Penn ; and all legislators, judges, and public officers had to declare and

---

[1] This is the information on the subject given by Madison in the "Debates of the Federal Convention," in the fifth and last vol. of Elliot's "Debates," p. 498. In the official "Journal of the Federal Convention," Elliot, vol. I., p. 277, it is simply stated that the clause, "but no religious test," etc., passed unanimously in the affirmative.

[2] "Commentaries on the Laws of England," Book IV. 59 and 439. Blackstone advocates limited toleration, and says (IV. 52) : "Certainly our ancestors were mistaken in their plans of compulsion and intolerance. The sin of schism, as such, is by no means the object of temporal coercion and punishment. . . . The magistrate is bound to protect the established church. . . . But, this point being once secured, all persecution for diversity of opinions, however ridiculous or absurd they may be, is contrary to every principle of sound policy and civil freedom."

subscribe their disbelief in transubstantiation, the adoration of the Virgin Mary and other saints, and the sacrifice of the Romish mass, as "superstitious and idolatrous," and their belief in the Holy Trinity and the divine inspiration of the Holy Scriptures. This test was in force from 1703 till the time of the Revolution, when, through the influence of Benjamin Franklin, it was removed from the State Constitution framed by the Convention of 1776. In Rhode Island, the Roman Catholics were deprived for a time of the right of voting, but this disqualification was no part of the original colonial charter, and is inconsistent with "the soul-liberty" of Roger Williams, the founder of that State.

The framers of the Federal Constitution, remembering the persecution of dissenters and nonconformists in the mother country and in several American colonies, cut the poisonous tree of persecution by the root, and substituted for specific religious tests a simple oath or solemn affirmation.

The discontent with state-churchism and its injustice toward dissenting convictions was one of the remote causes of the American Revolution.

THE FIRST AMENDMENT TO THE CONSTITUTION.

2. More important than this clause is the first amendment, which may be called the Magna Charta of religious freedom in the United States.[1]

The first amendment provides that " *Congress shall make no law respecting an establishment of religion, or prohibiting the free exercise thereof ;* or abridging the freedom of speech or of the press ; or the right of the people peaceably to assemble, and to petition the government for a redress of grievances."

This amendment is positive and protective, and consti-

---

[1] It is a serious defect of the two best histories of the American Constitution by George Ticknor Curtis (New York, Harper & Bro., 1854 and 1858, 2 vols.), and by George Bancroft (New York, D. Appleton & Co., third ed., 1883, 2 vols.), that they do not embrace a history of the amendments, which for our purpose is the most important.

tutes a bill of rights.   It prevents not only the establishment of a particular church, as the exclusive state-religion, but it expressly guarantees at the same time to all the churches the full liberty of religion in its public exercise, and forbids Congress ever to abridge this liberty.   Religious liberty is regarded as one of the fundamental and inalienable rights of an American citizen, and is associated with the liberty of speech and of the press, the right of peaceable assembly and of petition.

A large number of the most valuable provisions of the Magna Charta, which the clergy, the barons, and freemen of England wrung from the despotism of King John in 1215, and of the Bill of Rights, which was enacted against the despotism of the Stuarts in 1688, consist of the solemn recognitions of limitations upon the power of the Crown and the power of Parliament, such as the writ of habeas corpus, the right of trial by jury, the protection of life, liberty, and property from arbitrary spoliation, the right of petition, the right to bear arms, freedom of commerce. Several of these provisions are literally inserted among the amendments to our Constitution.   But it was left for America to abolish forever the tyranny of a state-religion, and to secure the most sacred of all rights and liberties to all her citizens—the liberty of religion and the free exercise thereof.

The United States furnishes the first example in history of a government deliberately depriving itself of all legislative control over religion, which was justly regarded by all older governments as the chief support of public morality, order, peace, and prosperity.   But it was an act of wisdom and justice rather than self-denial.   Congress was shut up to this course by the previous history of the American colonies and the actual condition of things at the time of the formation of the national government.   The Constitution did not create a nation, nor its religion and institutions.   It found them already existing, and was framed for the purpose of protecting them under a republican form of government, in a rule of the people, by the people, and for the people.

Nearly all the branches of the Christian Church were then represented in America. New England was settled by Congregationalists; Virginia, the Carolinas, and Georgia, by Episcopalians; New York, by Dutch Reformed, followed by Episcopalians; Rhode Island, by Baptists; Pennsylvania, by Quakers; Maryland, by Roman Catholics; while Presbyterians, Methodists, Lutherans, German Reformed, French Huguenots, Moravians, Mennonites, etc., were scattered through several colonies. In some States there was an established church; in others the mixed system of toleration prevailed. The Baptists and Quakers, who were victims of persecution and nurslings of adversity, professed full religious freedom as an article of their creed. All colonies, with the effectual aid of the churches and clergy, had taken part in the achievement of national independence, and had an equal claim to the protection of their rights and institutions by the national government.

The framers of the Constitution, therefore, had no right and no intention to interfere with the religion of the citizens of any State, or to discriminate between denominations; their only just and wise course was to leave the subject of religion with the several States, to put all churches on an equal footing before the national law, and to secure to them equal protection. Liberty of all is the best guarantee of the liberty of each.

North America was predestined from the very beginning for the largest religious and civil freedom, however imperfectly it was understood by the first settlers. It offered a hospitable home to emigrants of all nations and creeds. The great statesmen of the Philadelphia Convention recognized this providential destiny, and adapted the Constitution to it. They could not do otherwise. To assume the control of religion in any shape, except by way of protection, would have been an act of usurpation, and been stoutly resisted by all the States.

Thus Congress was led by Providence to establish a new system, which differed from that of Europe and the Colonies, and set an example to the several States for imitation.

THE ACTION OF THE STATE CONVENTIONS AND THE ORIGIN OF THE FIRST AMENDMENT.

The conventions of the several States, which were held in 1787 and 1788 for the ratification of the Federal Constitution, reflect the conflicting sentiments then entertained on the question of religious tests. At present nobody doubts the wisdom of that clause in the Constitution which removes such tests. "No provisions of the Constitution of the United States are more familiar to us," says a learned American historian,[1] "and more clearly express the universal sentiment of the American people, or are in more perfect harmony with the historic consciousness of the nation, than those which forbid the national government to establish any form of religion or to prescribe any religious test as a qualification for office held under its authority. Almost every other general principle of government embodied in that instrument has been discussed and argued about, and its application in particular cases resisted and questioned, until the intention of those who framed it seems lost in the Serbonian bog of controversy; yet no one has ever denied the rightfulness of the principle of religious liberty laid down in the Constitution."

But before the adoption of that instrument there was a wide difference of opinion on this, as well as on other articles. The exclusion of religious tests from qualification for public office under the general government was opposed in those States which required such tests, under the apprehension that without them the federal government might pass into the hands of Roman Catholics, Jews, and infidels. Even the Pope of Rome, said a delegate from North Carolina, might become President of the United States! On the other hand, several States, while adopting the Constitution, proposed amendments guaranteeing religious freedom and other fundamental rights.

The opposition to the abolition of religious tests was strongest in Massachusetts, where Congregationalism was

---

[1] Dr. Charles Stillé, "Religious Tests in Provincial Pennsylvania." A paper read before the Historical Society of Pennsylvania, November 9, 1885.

the established church.   Major Lusk, a delegate to the convention of that State, "shuddered at the idea that Romanists and pagans might be introduced into office, and that Popery and the Inquisition may be established in America.[1]"   But the Rev. Mr. Backus, in answer to this objection, remarked : " Nothing is more evident, both in reason and the Holy Scriptures, than that religion is ever a matter between God and individuals; and, therefore, no man or men can impose any religious test without invading the essential prerogatives of our Lord Jesus Christ. . . . Imposing of religious tests has been the greatest engine of tyranny in the world. . . . Some serious minds discover a concern lest if all religious tests should be excluded the Congress would hereafter establish Popery or some other tyrannical way of worship.   But it is most certain that no such way of worship can be established without any religious tests." [2]   The same clergyman spoke strongly against slavery, which " grows more and more odious in the world," and expressed the hope that, though it was not struck with apoplexy by the proposed Constitution, it would die with consumption by the prohibition of the importation of slaves after a certain date (1808).   The Rev. Mr. Shute was equally pronounced in his defence of the clause.   "To establish a religious test," [3] he said," as a qualification for offices would be attended with injurious consequences to some individuals, and with no advantage to the whole. . . . Unprincipled and dishonest men will not hesitate to subscribe to any thing. . . . Honest men alone, however well qualified to serve the public, would be excluded by the test, and their country be deprived of the benefit of their abilities.   In this great and extensive empire there   is, and will be, a great variety of sentiments in religion among its inhabitants. . . . Whatever answer bigotry may suggest, the dictates of candor and equity will be: no religious tests. . . .   I believe that there are worthy characters among men of every denomination—among Quakers, Baptists, the Church of England,

---

[1] Elliot's " Debates," vol. II. 148.   [2] *Ibid.,* II. 148 *sq.*
[3] *Ibid.,* II. 118 *sq.*

the Papists, and even among those who have no other guide in the way of virtue and heaven than the dictates of natural religion. . . . The Apostle Peter tells us that God is no respecter of persons, but, in every nation, he that feareth him and worketh righteousness is acceptable to him. And I know of no reason why men of such a character, in a community of whatever denomination in religion, *cæteris paribus*, with other suitable qualifications, should not be acceptable to the people, and why they may not be employed by them with safety and advantage in the important offices of government." The Rev. Mr. Payson spoke in the same strain, and insisted that "human tribunals for the consciences of men are impious encroachments upon the prerogatives of God."[1] It is very evident that these Congregational ministers of the gospel represented the true American spirit in the convention, rather than Major Lusk and Colonel Jones, who favored religious tests. The Convention of Massachusetts ratified the Constitution, February 7, 1788, by a majority of 19 (187 to 168), with proposition of 9 alternatives and provisions which, however, do not include religious liberty, unless it be implied in the first proposition: "That it be explicitly understood that all powers not expressly delegated by the aforesaid Constitution are reserved to the several States to be by them exercised."

In the Convention of North Carolina, held July, 1788, the same fear was expressed, that, without some religious tests, Jews, infidels, and Papists might get into offices of trust, but Mr. Iredell said, that "under the color of religious tests the utmost cruelties have been exercised," and that America has set an example "of moderation and general religious liberty. Happily no sect here is superior to another. As long as this is the case, we shall be free from those persecutions with which other countries have been torn." Among the twenty amendments proposed by North Carolina as a "declaration of rights," and put on record, the last is this, which literally agrees with one proposed by Virginia:

[1] *Ibid.*, ii. 120.

" That religion, or the duty which we owe to our Creator, and the manner of discharging it, can be directed only by reason and conviction, not by force or violence, and, therefore, all men have an equal, natural, and unalienable right to the free exercise of religion, according to the dictates of conscience ; and that no particular religious sect or society ought to be favored or established by law in preference to others." [1]

North Carolina did not ratify the Constitution till November 21, 1789.

In Virginia the exclusion of religious tests was regarded by the advanced liberal party as quite insufficient, and a more explicit guarantee against the establishment of a religion was demanded. In that State the Church of England had been disestablished, and full liberty secured to all forms of belief, by an act of October, 1785, two years before the framing of the Federal Constitution.[2]

This act was brought about by the combined influence of the dissenters (Presbyterians, Baptists, Quakers, etc.), who formed at that time two thirds of the population, and the political school of Jefferson, who was of Episcopalian descent, but had early imbibed the Voltaireian philosophy of toleration, and during his residence in Paris (1784–1789) had intimately associated with the leaders of French infidelity. He composed the Declaration of Independence (1776), but had nothing to do with the framing of the Federal Constitution (being then absent in France). He was opposed to centralization, both as Secretary of State, in Washington's first cabinet, and, with more moderation, as President. He founded the Anti-Federalist party and the State Rights theory, which afterwards logically developed into the Nullifica-

---

[1] Elliot, vol. iv. 242, 244. Comp. p. 192, and iii. 659.

[2] That act, after fully setting forth strong arguments against state-churchism and intolerance, declares : " *Be it therefore enacted by the General Assembly,* that no man shall be compelled to frequent or support any religious worship, place, or ministry whatsoever, nor shall be enforced, restrained, molested, or burthened in his body or goods, nor shall otherwise suffer on account of his religious opinions or belief ; but that all men shall be free to profess, and by argument to maintain, their opinions in matters of religion, and that the same shall in no wise diminish, enlarge, or affect their civil capacities." " Collection of the Laws of Virginia by W. W. Hening," vol. xii. p. 84 (Richmond, 1823). Ten years before, in 1776, the oppressive acts against dissenters had been repealed.

tion theory of Calhoun, and the Secession theory of Jefferson Davis, but he differed from his southern successors by his decided opposition to the institution of slavery. He was no member of the Convention of Richmond in 1788, but his influence was thrown against the adoption of the Constitution without " a declaration of rights which shall stipulate freedom of religion, freedom of the press, freedom of commerce against monopolies, trial by juries in all cases, no suspensions of the habeas corpus, no standing armies." [1] Patrick Henry, also, who was a member of that Convention, violently opposed the adoption of the Constitution without a bill of rights.[2] On the guarantee for freedom of religion, all parties of Virginia were agreed, except that some of the leading men, including Washington and Patrick Henry, favored the taxing of the people for the support of some church of their preference. The Convention, therefore, recommended to Congress, among other amendments, the following :

[1] See his letter to A. Donald, dated Paris, Febr. 7, 1788, in " The Writings of Th. Jefferson " (N. York, 1853), vol. ii. 355. In a letter to the Danbury Baptist Association, Jan. 1, 1802, he expressed his great satisfaction with the First Amendment. " Believing with you," he says, "that religion is a matter which lies solely between man and his God, that he owes account to none other for his faith or his worship, that the legislative powers of government reach actions only, and not opinions, I contemplate with sovereign reverence that act of the whole American people, which declared that their legislature should ' make no law, respecting an establishment of religion or prohibiting the free exercise thereof,' thus building a wall of separation between church and state." Vol. viii. 113. His gives his views on religious freedom in his " Notes on the State of Virginia," 1787, Ch. 17. Comp. Randall's " Life of Thomas Jefferson," vol. iii. 553–558. Jefferson was a Unitarian, but he generally attended the Episcopal church, carried his prayer-book, and joined in the responses. He contributed liberally to churches, Bible societies, and other religious objects. See Randall, iii. 555. He concludes his first inaugural, March 4, 1801, with the prayer : " May that infinite Power which rules the destinies of the universe, lead our councils to what is best, and give them a favorable issue for our peace and prosperity." And in the course of his address he alludes to our " benign religion " and the " overruling Providence," as the best security of our happiness and prosperity. This is very vague, indeed, but there are few Christian rulers of modern Europe who go even so far in their official utterances.

[2] See his speeches in Elliot, iii. 593 *sqq.*

" That religion, or the duty which we owe to our Creator, and the manner of discharging it, can be directed only by reason and conviction, not by force or violence ; and therefore all men have an equal, natural, and unalienable right to the free exercise of religion, according to the dictates of conscience, and that no particular religious sect or society ought to be favored or established by law in preference to others." [1]

This amendment is substantially a repetition of article 16th in the " Declaration of Rights," which was prepared by Thomas Jefferson, and unanimously adopted by the Legislature of Virginia, June 12, 1776 (several weeks before the Declaration of Independence, July 4, 1776), and reads as follows :

" That religion, or the duty which we owe to our Creator, and the manner of discharging it, can be directed only by reason and conviction, not by force or violence, and therefore all men are equally entitled to the free exercise of religion, according to the dictates of conscience ; and that it is the mutual duty of all to practice Christian forbearance, love, and charity, towards each other." [2]

New Hampshire proposed twelve alterations, the eleventh of which is :

" Congress shall make no laws touching religion, or to infringe the rights of conscience." [3]

The Convention of New York, held in Poughkeepsie, June 17–July 26, 1788, adopted the Constitution after excited debates, in which Governor Clinton, Alexander Hamilton, Robert R. Livingston, John Jay, Melancthon Smith, and Mr. Lansing took prominent part, with a majority of only three (30 to 27), and with sundry recommendations and principles, among which is this :

" That the people have an equal, natural, and unalienable right freely and peaceably to exercise their religion according to the dictates of conscience ; and that no religious sect or society ought to be favored or established by law in preference to others." [4]

The State of New York had virtually disestablished the Episcopal Church in 1777, one year after the Declaration of Independence, by repealing, in its constitution, all statutes and acts of the colony which " might be construed to estab-

---

[1] Elliot, iii. 659.

[2] Hening's " Collection of the Laws of Virginia," vol. ix. p. 111. The words " are equally entitled," were changed into " have *an equal, natural, and unalienable right*," and the same phraseology was used by the North Carolina, New York, and Rhode Island Conventions. I am unable to trace its precise origin.   [3] Elliot, i. 326.   [4] Elliot, i. 328.

lish or maintain any particular denomination of Christians and their ministers " ; and it ordained that " the free exercise and enjoyment of religious profession and worship, without discrimination or preference, shall forever hereafter be allowed within this State to all mankind." [1]

Pennsylvania ratified the Constitution December 12, 1787, by a majority of fifteen, but the dissenting minority, failing to secure a new national convention, issued an address to their constituents, called " Reasons of Dissent," etc., in which fourteen amendments were proposed, the first being a guarantee of religious freedom in these words :

" The right of conscience shall be held inviolable, and neither the legislative, executive, nor judicial powers of the United States shall have authority to alter, abrogate, or infringe any part of the constitutions of the several States, which provide for the preservation of liberty in matters of religion." [2]

Rhode Island was the last to ratify the Constitution, May 29, 1790, and then only with a prefatory declaration of eighteen principles, the fourth of which is in almost verbal agreement with the declaration of Virginia as follows :

" That religion, or the duty which we owe to our Creator, and the manner of discharging it, can be directed only by reason and conviction, and not by force and violence ; and therefore all men have a natural, equal, and unalienable right to the exercise of religion according to the dictates of conscience ; and that no particular religious sect or society ought to be favored or established, by law, in preference to others." [3]

To the ratification were added seventeen amendments as recommendations, but religious liberty is not included.

The First Congress of the United States met under the Constitution March 4, 1789. In the session of June 8th, the House of Representatives, on motion of James Madison, of Virginia, took into consideration the amendments to the Constitution desired by several States, and resolved itself into a committee of the whole. After much useless debate, Mr. Madison moved the appointment of a select committee to report proper amendments, and supported it by a long

[1] See Murray Hoffman, " Ecclesiast. Law of the State of New York." N. Y. 1868, p. 40.

[2] " The Reasons of Dissent " were published, Philadelphia, Dec. 12, 1787, and reprinted in Carey's " American Museum," vol. ii. No. V. pp. 536–553.

[3] *Elliot*, i. 334.

and strong speech, urging as a reason chiefly the duty of Congress to remove all apprehensions of an intention to deprive the people " of the liberty for which they valiantly sought and honorably bled." " I believe," he said, " that the great mass of the people who opposed the Constitution disliked it because it did not contain effectual provisions against encroachments on particular rights, and those safeguards which they have been long accustomed to have interposed between them and the magistrate who exercises the sovereign power ; nor ought we to consider them safe, while a great number of our fellow-citizens think these securities necessary." He then proposed nine amendments, and among these the following, which bears directly on our subject :

" Fourthly, That in article I., section 9, between clauses 3 and 4, be inserted these clauses, to wit : The civil rights of none shall be abridged on account of religious belief or worship, nor shall any national religion be established, nor shall the full and equal rights of conscience be in any manner, or on any pretext, infringed."

Under the same head Madison mentioned the guarantees of the freedom of speech and the press, and the right to petition, which are included in the First Amendment as it now stands.

Much opposition was made to such amendments, chiefly on the ground that they were unnecessary in a free republic. In the session of July 21st a select committee of representatives of the eleven States which had adopted the Constitution, consisting of Messrs. Vining, Madison, Baldwin, Sherman, Burke, Gillman Cymer, Benson, Goodhue, Boudinot, and Gale, was appointed " to take the subject of amendments to the Constitution of the United States generally into their consideration, and to report thereupon to the House."

The report was discussed and amended. On August 24, 1789, the House adopted a series of amendments and ordered the clerk to send them to the Senate, which agreed to some, and objected to others. The two Houses came to an agreement on the 25th of September, 1789.[1]

[1] The authority for these statements on the proceedings of the First Congress bearing on our subject, see in the " Annals of Congress " (ed. by Jos. Gales), Washington, 1834, vol. i. pp. 440 *sqq. ;* 448 *sqq. ;* 685–692 ; 699 ; 730 *sqq. ;*

Congress accordingly sent twelve amendments to the Legislatures of the several States for ratification, three fourths being necessay for the purpose.[1] The first two, relating to the number of representatives (Art. I.), and to compensation for services of the senators and representatives (Art. II.), were rejected by some, the other ten were duly ratified by all the Legislatures except those of Massachusetts, Connecticut, and Georgia, which made no returns, and by silence gave consent.[2]

796 *sqq.* 758. On page 951 the "Annals" report : "A message from the Senate informed the House that the Senate agree to the amendment proposed by this House to their amendments to the several articles of amendment to the Constitution of the United States." In the same session of September 25th, Mr. Boudinot moved a resolution to request the President to recommend "a day of public thanksgiving and prayer for the many signal favors of Almighty God, especially by affording the people an opportunity peaceably to establish a constitution of government for their safety and happiness." The resolution was objected to by Tucker, but supported by Sherman, and adopted.

[1] Elliot's "Debates," i. 338 and 339. The preamble states :

"The conventions of a number of States having, at the time of their adopting the Constitution, expressed a desire, in order to prevent misconstruction or abuse of its powers, that further declaratory and restrictive clauses should be added ; and as extending the ground of public confidence in the government will best insure the beneficent ends of its institution :—

"*Resolved, by the Senate and House of Representatives of the United States of America, in Congress assembled,* two thirds of both Houses concurring, that the following articles be proposed to the legislatures of the several States, as amendments to the Constitution of the United States, all or any of which articles, when ratified by three fourths of the said legislatures, to be valid, to all intents and purposes, as part of said Constitution, namely,—"

Then follow the twelve articles. The document is signed by FREDERICK AUGUSTUS MUHLENBERG, Speaker of the House of Representatives, and by JOHN ADAMS, Vice-President of the United States and President of the Senate.

[2] In the "Annals of Congress," ii. 2033, are recorded the ratifications of New Hampshire (Jan. 25, 1790, all except Art. II.) ; New York (Feb. 24, 1790, except Arts. I. and II.) ; Pennsylvania (March 11, 1790, except Arts. I. and II.) ; Delaware, Jan. 28, 1790, all but Art. I.) ; Maryland, Dec. 19, 1789, all ; South Carolina (Jan. 19, 1790, all) ; North Carolina (Dec. 22, 1789, all) ; Rhode Island (June, 1790, except Art. II.) ; New Jersey (Nov. 20, all but Art. II.). In the Annals of the Second Congress, Oct. 24, 1791 to Mar. 2, 1793 (Washington, 1849), pp. 54 and 75, is reported the ratification of Virginia (Dec. 5, 1791, except Art. I.), and of Vermont (Nov. 3, 1791, all). There is no record on the journals of Congress that the legislatures of Connecticut, Massachusetts, and Georgia ratified the amendments. They were declared in force by the Proclamation of Washington December 15, 1791.

Thus the first ten of the amendments became part and parcel of the Constitution in 1791. The first of them (which was originally the third) is the guarantee of religious liberty.

From these facts it appears that the credit of the First Amendment is due to the First Congress, which proposed it, and to the conventions of the States of New York, Virginia, North Carolina, Rhode Island, New Hampshire, and the minority of Pennsylvania, all of which suggested it, directly or indirectly, in substantially the same language.

As to individuals, James Madison, of Virginia, who became the fourth President of the United States, has the honor of being the chief advocate of this amendment in Congress. It was his conviction that religion was the gainer by its separation from politics. We have an interesting testimony to this effect from his pen in a letter to Edward Livingston, dated Montpellier, July 10, 1822. "It was the belief of all sects at one time," he says, "that the establishment of religion by law was right and necessary; that the true religion ought to be established in exclusion of every other; and that the only question to be decided was, which was the true religion. The example of Holland proved that a toleration of sects dissenting from the established sect was safe, and even useful. The example of the colonies, now States, which rejected religious establishments altogether, proved that all sects might be safely and advantageously put on a footing of equal and entire freedom. . . . It is impossible to deny that in Virginia religion prevails with more zeal and a more exemplary priesthood than it ever did when established and patronized by public authority. We are teaching the world the great truth that governments do better without kings and nobles than with them. The merit will be doubled by the other lesson: that religion flourishes in greater purity without than with the aid of government."[1]

[1] " Letters and Other Writings of James Madison, Fourth President of the United States," in 4 vols., published by order of Congress, Philadelphia, 1867. vol. iii. 275, 276.

LIMITATION OF RELIGIOUS LIBERTY—DECISION OF THE UNITED STATES SUPREME COURT ON MORMON POLYG-AMY.

The Constitution does not define "religion," nor limit "the free exercise thereof." But "religion" must, at all events, include all branches of the Christian Church which then existed in the various States, with their creeds, forms of government, worship, and discipline. They are all excluded from becoming a state-religion, but all can practise and enjoy "free exercise." This is much more than freedom of religious *opinions;* for this exists everywhere, even under the most despotic governments, and is beyond the reach of law, which deals only with overt actions. Freedom of exercise includes public worship, acts of discipline, and every legitimate manifestation of religion.

The spirit and disposition of our government allow the widest latitude to this free exercise that is at all consistent with public safety. Hence even irreligion and infidelity have free play and scatter their poison wide and far by word and pen. The prevailing sentiment is, that error may safely be tolerated where truth is free to combat it. Truth is mighty and must prevail in the end. Its triumph is all the more sure and lasting if it is brought about by its own merits, unaided by material force.

But there must be some boundary to religious, as to all other liberty, when it assumes an organized shape or manifests itself in public acts. Liberty is not lawlessness and licentiousness. No man has the liberty to do wrong, or to injure his neighbor, or to endanger the public peace and welfare. Liberty, in the nature of the case, is limited by the supreme law of self-preservation, which inheres in a commonwealth as well as in an individual; and by the golden rule of loving our neighbor as ourselves. My neighbor's liberty is as sacred as mine, and I dare not encroach upon it. Religious liberty may be abused as well as the liberty of speech and of the press, or any other liberty; and all abuses are punishable by law if they violate the rights of others. A religion which injures *public morals* and enjoins *criminal practices* is a public nuisance, and must be treated as such.

So far religious liberty in America has moved within the bounds of Christian civilization and public morality, and it is not likely to transgress those bounds.

The first and so far the only case in which the government was forced to define the limits of religious liberty was the case of Mormon polygamy in Utah, which is sanctioned by the Mormon religion, but which is utterly opposed to Western, as distinct from Oriental, civilization. The Congress of the United States prohibited polygamy by law (1862).[1] The Supreme Court sustained the prohibition as constitutional and valid, and within the legislative power of Congress which has exclusive control over the Territories. In the decision, delivered October, 1878, Chief-Justice Morrison R. Waite thus defines the bounds of the religious liberty guaranteed by the Constitution:[2]

"Laws are made for the government of actions, and while they cannot interfere with mere religious belief and opinions, they may with practices. Suppose one believed that human sacrifices were a necessary part of religious worship, would

---

[1] Section 5352 of the Revised Statutes : " Every person having a husband or wife living, who marries another, whether married or single, in a Territory or other place over which the United States have exclusive jurisdiction, is guilty of bigamy, and shall be punished by a fine of not more than $500, and by imprisonment for a term of not more than five years."

[2] *Reynolds* vs. *the United States*, vol. 98, U. S. Supreme Court Reports, p. 166 *sqq.* The plaintiff, George Reynolds, was charged with bigamy, and "proved that at the time of his alleged second marriage he was a member of the Church of Jesus Christ of Latter-Day Saints, commonly called the Mormon Church, and a believer in its doctrines ; that it was an accepted doctrine of that church, that it was the duty of male members of said church, circumstances permitting, to practise polygamy ; . . . that this duty was enjoined by different books which the members of said church believed to be of divine origin, and among others the Holy Bible, and also that the members of the church believed that the practice of polygamy was directly enjoined upon the male members thereof by the Almighty God, in a revelation to Joseph Smith, the founder and prophet of said church ; that the failing or refusing to practise polygamy by such male members of said church, when circumstances would admit, would be punished, and that the penalty for such failure and refusal would be damnation in the life to come." (P. 161.)

it be seriously contended that the civil government under which he lived could not interfere to prevent a sacrifice? Or if a wife religiously believed it was her duty to burn herself upon the funeral pile of her dead husband, would it be beyond the power of the civil government to prevent her carrying her belief into practice?

"So here, as a law of the organization of society under the exclusive dominion of the United States, it is provided that plural marriages shall not be allowed. Can a man exercise his practices to the contrary because of his religious belief? To permit this would be to make the professed doctrines of religious belief superior to the law of the land, and in effect to permit every citizen to become a law unto himself. Government could exist only in name under such circumstances."

This decision is of the greatest importance. It would strictly exclude from toleration also the public exercise of Mohammedanism which sanctions polygamy, and of such heathen religions as sanction human sacrifices.

The popular hostility to the Chinese in California, and the congressional restriction of Chinese immigration, are partly due to American intolerance of the heathen customs and practices of that remarkable people, who, by their industry and skill, have largely contributed to the development of the material wealth of the Pacific States, and deserve a better treatment than they have received.

How far the United States government may go hereafter in the limitations of religious liberty depends upon the course of public opinion, which frames and interprets the laws in a free country.

The constitutions of the individual States, which guarantee religious liberty, generally guard it against abuse, and expressly declare that "the liberty of conscience hereby secured shall not be so construed as to excuse acts of licentiousness, or justify practices inconsistent with the peace and safety of the State."[1]

---

[1] So the constitutions of New York, Illinois, California, and other States.

THE CHARGE OF POLITICAL ATHEISM.

The colonial charters, the Declaration of Independence, and most of the State constitutions recognize, more or less explicitly, the great truth of an all-ruling Providence in the origin and history of nations. But the Constitution of the United States omits the mention even of the name of God.[1]

This was a sin of omission, if sin at all, but not of commission, or intentional slight. Washington, in his reply to a Christian address from Massachusetts and New Hampshire after his inauguration, ascribes the absence of any regulation respecting religion to the consideration of the framers that " this important object is more properly committed to the guidance of the ministers of the gospel." [2]

The omission or inadvertency has given rise to the charge of political atheism against the Constitution.

During the civil war, when the religious sensibilities of the nation were excited in their inmost depths, and the fate of the Union was trembling in the balance, a " National Association to secure certain religious amendments to the Constitution " was formed under the presidency of Justice William Strong, of the United States Supreme Court, for the purpose of carrying through Congress such an alteration in the preamble as would recognize the national faith in God and in Christ. The amendment is as follows, the proposed insertions being included in brackets :

" We, the people of the United States [humbly acknowledging Almighty God as the source of all authority and power in civil government, the Lord Jesus Christ as the Ruler of all nations, and his revealed will as the supreme law of the land, in order to constitute a Christian government, and] in order

---

[1] So did also the Articles of Confederation of July 24, 1778, except in the words of the Ratification : " Whereas it has pleased the Great Governor of the world," etc.

[2] B. F. Morris, " Christian Life and Character of the Civil Institutions of the United States" (Philadelphia, 1864), p. 248, reports a mythical story of Alexander Hamilton, that after the adjournment of the Convention he was asked the reason of the omission by Rev. Dr. Miller, of Princeton, and replied : " I declare we forgot it." But Dr. Miller was not called to Princeton till 1813, nine years after Hamilton's death. Morris gives no authority for his statement, and introduces it simply by a vague " it is said."

to form a more perfect union, establish justice, ensure domestic tranquility, provide for the common defence, promote the general welfare, and secure the [inalienable rights and] blessings of [life], liberty, [and the pursuit of happiness] to ourselves and our posterity [and all the inhabitants of the land], do ordain and establish this Constitution for the United States of America." [1]

These additions in the preamble, or enacting clause, to be operative, would require a special provision in the Constitution itself, giving Congress the power, by appropriate legislation, to gain the proposed end of establishing "a Christian government," and to forbid, under penalties, the public exercise of non-Christian religions. This, again, would require an alteration or express limitation of the First Amendment to the various forms of Christianity. There is no prospect that such an amendment can ever command a majority in Congress and the Legislatures of the States. The best chance was passed when the amendments suggested by the war and the emancipation of the slaves were enacted. The Constitution of the Confederate States, framed at Montgomery, Alabama, during the civil war (March 11, 1861), actually did insert Almighty God in the preamble, but that constitution died with the Confederacy in 1865. The name of God did not make it more pious or justifiable. [2]

Our chief objection to such an amendment, besides its impracticability, is that it rests on a false assumption, and casts an unjust reflection upon the original document, as if it were hostile to religion. But it is neither hostile nor

[1] See "Proceedings of the National Convention to secure the Religious Amendment to the Constitution of the U. S. held at Cincinnati, Jan. 31 and Feb. 1, 1872." Philadelphia, 1872. Another national convention was held in New York, February 1873. Compare, also, the previous and subsequent publications of that Association, and their semi-monthly journal, "The Christian Statesman," Philadelphia.

[2] The Confederate Constitution follows the Federal Constitution very closely, but provides for the theory of State Rights and for the protection of the institution of slavery, which caused the civil war. The preamble reads as follows (with the characteristic words in italics) : "We, the people of the *Confederate* [instead of *United*] States, *each State acting in its sovereign and independent character*, in order to form *a permanent federal government* [instead of *a more perfect union*], establish justice, insure domestic tranquillity, and secure the blessings of liberty to ourselves and our posterity—*invoking the favor and guidance of Almighty God*—ordain and establish this Constitution of the *Con-*

friendly to any religion ; it is simply silent on the subject, as
lying beyond the jurisdiction of the general government.
The absence of the names of God and Christ, in a purely
political and legal document, no more proves denial or
irreverence than the absence of those names in a mathemati-
cal treatise, or the statutes of a bank or railroad corporation.
The title " Holiness" does not make the Pope of Rome any
holier than he is, and it makes the contradiction only more
glaring in such characters as Alexander VI.   The book of
Esther and the Song of Solomon are undoubtedly produc-
tions of devout worshippers of Jehovah ; and yet the name of
God does not occur once in them.

We may go further and say that the Constitution not only
contains nothing which is irreligious or unchristian, but is
Christian in substance, though not in form.   It is per-
vaded by the spirit of justice and humanity, which are
Christian.   The First Amendment could not have originated in any pagan or Mohammedan country, but presup-
poses Christian civilization and culture.   Christianity alone
has taught men to respect the sacredness of the human
personality as made in the image of God and redeemed by
Christ, and to protect its rights and privileges, including the
freedom of worship, against the encroachments of the temporal power and the absolutism of the state.

The Constitution, moreover, in recognizing and requiring
an official oath from the President and all legislative, executive, and judicial officers, both of the United States and of
the several States, recognizes the Supreme Being, to whom
the oath is a solemn appeal.   In exempting Sunday from
the working days of the President for signing a bill of Congress, the Constitution honors the claims of the weekly day
of rest and the habits of a Sunday-keeping nation ; and in

federate [for *United*] States of America."   Jefferson Davis, in discussing the
alleged improvements of the Confederate Constitution, does not deem this
religious clause worth mentioning.   See his "The Rise and Fall of the Confederate Government" (New York, Appleton & Co., 1881), vol. i. p. 259.   In
appendix K. (pp. 648 *sqq*.), he gives the text of both Constitutions in parallel
columns.   The Confederate Constitution retains the third clause of Art VI. and
transfers the First Amendment to section 9 of Article I.

the subscription, by the words " in the year of our Lord," it assents to that chronology which implies that Jesus Christ is the turning-point of history and the beginning of a new order of society.

And, finally, the framers of the Constitution were, without exception, believers in God and in future rewards and punishments, from the presiding officer, General Washington, who was a communicant member of the Episcopal Church, down to the least orthodox, Dr. Benjamin Franklin, who was affected by the spirit of English deism and French infidelity, but retained a certain reverence for the religion of his Puritan ancestors. All recognized the hand of Divine Providence in leading them safely through the war of independence. Dr. Franklin, in an eloquent and highly creditable speech, proposed the employment of a chaplain in the Convention, who should invoke the wisdom and blessing of God upon the responsible work of framing laws for a new nation.[1]

The history of the general government sustains our interpretation. The only example of an apparent hostility to Christianity is the treaty with Tripoli, November 4, 1796, in which it is said—perhaps unguardedly and unnecessarily— that the government of the United States is "not founded on the Christian religion," and has no enmity against the religion of a Mohammedan nation.[2] But this treaty was signed

[1] See Document III. It is noteworthy that President Cleveland incorporated this address of Franklin in his eulogy of the Constitution at the Centennial celebration in Philadelphia, Sept. 17, 1887.

[2] " As the government of the United States of America is *not in any sense founded on the Christian religion ;* as it has in itself no character of enmity against the laws, religion, or tranquillity of Musselmen ; and as the said States never have entered into any war or act of hostility against any Mahometan nation, it is declared by the parties, that no pretext arising from religious opinions shall ever produce an interruption of the harmony existing between the two countries." Article XI. of Treaty with Tripoli, signed and sealed at Tripoli Nov. 4, 1796, and at Algiers, Jan. 3, 1797, by Hassan Bashan (Dey of Algiers) and Joel Barlow (Consul-Gen. of the U. S.). See " Treaties and Conventions conducted between the U. S. and other Powers," Washington, 1873, p. 838. I learn from Dr. Francis Wharton that the treaty was framed by an ex-Congregational clergyman. With this treaty should be compared the treaties with Turkey which protest the rights of American Missionaries.

by Washington, who could not mean thereby to slight the
religion he himself professed.   It simply means that the
United States is founded, like all civil governments, in the
law of nature, and not hostile to any religion.   Man, as
Aristotle says, is by nature a political animal.[1]   Civil government belongs to the kingdom of the Father, not of the
Son.   Paul recognized the Roman Empire under Nero as
founded by God, and that empire persecuted the Christian
religion for nearly three hundred years.   The modern German Empire and the French Republic arose, like the United
States, from purely secular motives, but are not on that
account irreligious or anti - Christian.   The Constitution
(*Verfassungsurkunde*) of the German Empire proclaimed by
the Emperor William, April 16, 1861, has in its seventy-
eight articles not a single allusion to religion, except in the
title of the Emperor *von Gottes Gnaden*, and might with much
more justice be declared an atheistic document than the Constitution of the United States.

It is easy to make a plausible logical argument in favor of
the proposition that the state cannot be neutral, that no-re-
ligion is irreligion, and that non-Christian is anti-Christian.
But facts disprove the logic.   The world is full of happy and
unhappy inconsistencies.   Christ says, indeed, " Who is not
for me is against me," but he says also, with the same right,
"Who is not against me is for me."   It is the latter, and not
the former truth which applies to the American state, as is
manifest from its history down to the present time.   A mere
verbal recognition of God and Christ might be construed as
an empty patronizing formality.   Having the substance, we
may dispense with the shadow, which might cast suspicion
upon the reality.

See the instruction of Secretary Bayard to Straus, April 20, 1887, in which he
says : " It is with peculiar satisfaction that the department learns that, in
part through the instrumentality of Mr. Pendleton King as chargé d'affaires,
an arrangement has been effected with the Turkish authorities by which the
[American] missions are enabled to pursue, as heretofore, their meritorious,
unselfish, and beneficent work among Turks in Turkey."—Appendix to vol. iii.
of " Digest of International Law," by Francis Wharton, LL.D., Washington, 1887, p. 864.

[1] ἄνθρωπος φύσει πολιτικὸν (staatlich) ζῶον. " Polit." Bk I. ch. 2.

Our Constitution, as all free government, is based upon popular sovereignty. This is a fact which no one can deny. But this fact by no means excludes the higher fact that all government and power on earth are of divine origin, dependent on God's will and responsible to him (Rom. xiii., 1). God can manifest his will through the voice of the people fully as well as through the election of princes or nobles, or through the accident of birth. In the ancient church even bishops (like Cyprian, Ambrose, Augustin) and popes (like Gregory the Great) were chosen by the people, and the *vox populi* was accepted as the *vox Dei*. When these come in conflict, we must obey God rather than man (Acts iv., 29). All power, parental, civil, and ecclesiastical, is liable to abuse in the hands of sinful men, and if government commands us to act against conscience and right, disobedience, and, if necessary, revolution, becomes a necessity and a duty.

THE INFIDEL PROGRAM.

A direct opposition to the efforts of the " National Association to Secure a Religious Amendment to the Constitution of the United States " is an attempt of the " Liberal League " to expunge from it every trace of Christianity. The former aims to christianize the Constitution and to nationalize Christianity; the latter aims to heathenize the Constitution and to denationalize Christianity.

The program of the " Liberal League," as published by Francis E. Abbot, in their organ, *The Index*, January 4, 1873, and separately, is as follows:

" THE DEMANDS OF LIBERALISM.

" 1. We demand that churches and other ecclesiastical property shall no longer be exempted from just taxation.

" 2. We demand that the employment of chaplains in Congress, in State Legislatures, in the navy and militia, and in prisons, asylums, and all other institutions supported by public money, shall be discontinued.

" 3. We demand that all public appropriations for sectarian, educational, and charitable institutions shall cease.

" 4. We demand that all religious services now sustained by the government shall be abolished ; and especially that the use of the Bible in the public schools, whether ostensibly as a text-book, or avowedly as a book of religious worship, shall be prohibited.

" 5. We demand that the appointment, by the President of the United States- or by the Governors of the various States, of all religious festivals and feasts shall wholly cease.

" 6. We demand that the judicial oath in the courts, and in all other departments of the government, shall be abolished, and that simple affirmation under pains and penalties of perjury shall be established in its stead.

" 7. We demand that all laws, directly or indirectly, enforcing the observance of Sunday as the Sabbath shall be repealed.

" 8. We demand that all laws looking to the enforcement of ' Christian morality shall be abrogated, and that all laws shall be conformed to the requirements of natural morality, equal rights, and impartial liberty.

" 9. We demand that not only in the Constitutions of the United States and of the several States, but also in the practical administration of the same, no privilege or advantage shall be conceded to Christianity or any other special religion ; that our entire political system shall be founded and administered on a purely secular basis ; and that whatever changes shall prove necessary to this end shall be consistently, unflinchingly, and promptly made.

" Liberals ! I pledge to you my undivided sympathies and most vigorous co-operation, both in *The Index* and out of it, in this work of local and national organization. Let us begin at once to lay the foundations of a great national party of freedom, which shall demand the entire secularization of our municipal, State, and national government.

" Let us boldly and with high purpose meet the duty of the hour. Rouse, then, to the great work of freeing America from the usurpations of the Church ! Make this continent from ocean to ocean sacred to human liberty ! Prove that you are worthy descendants of those whose wisdom and patriotism gave us a Constitution untainted with superstitution ! Shake off your slumbers, and break the chains to which you have too long tamely submitted."

There are some good religious people who from entirely different motives and aims sympathize with a part of this program, under the mistaken notion that the separation of church and state must be absolute, and requires, as its logical result, the exclusion of the Bible and all religious teaching from the public schools. But an absolute separation is an impossibility, as we have seen already and shall show hereafter.

The state cannot be divorced from morals, and morals cannot be divorced from religion. The state is more in need of the moral support of the church than the church is in need of the protection of the state. What will become of a state, or a school, which is indifferent to the fundamental virtues of honesty, integrity, justice, temperance? And how can these, or any other virtues, be more effectually maintained and promoted than by the solemn sanctions of religion which binds man to God? We will not speak of the graces of humility, chastity, and charity, which were and are unknown before and outside of revelation. The second table of the Ten Commandments is based upon the first. Love to man is impossible without love to God, who first loved us.

If the aim of the "National Association" is impracticable, the aim of the "Liberal League" is tenfold more impracticable. The change in the preamble of the Constitution would be an easy task compared with the task of expelling the Christian religion from the national life. To carry out their program, the Free-thinkers would have to revolutionize public sentiment, to alter the constitutions and laws of the country, to undo or repudiate our whole history, to unchristianize the nation, and sink it below the heathen standard. For the wisest among the heathen acknowledged the necessity of religion as the basis of the commonwealth. Socrates said to Alcibiades, according to Plato: "To act justly and wisely, you must act according to the will of God." Plutarch, the purest and noblest of the Platonists, in a work against an Epicurean philosopher (*Adv. Colotem*), makes the remarkable statement: "There never was a state of atheists. You may travel all over the world, and you may find cities without walls, without king, without mint, without theatre or gymnasium; but you will nowhere find a city without a God, without prayer, without oracle, without sacrifice. Sooner may a city stand without foundations, than a state without belief in the gods. This is the bond of all society, and the pillar of all legislation."

THE STATE CONSTITUTIONS.

The Federal Constitution did not abolish the union of church and state where it previously existed, nor does it forbid any of the States to establish a religion or to favor a particular church. It leaves them free to deal with religion as they please, provided only they do not deprive any American citizen of his right to worship God according to his conscience. It does not say: "*No State* shall make a law respecting an establishment of religion"; nor: "*Neither* Congress *nor* any State," etc., but simply: "*Congress* shall make no law," etc.   The States retained every power, jurisdiction, and right which they had before, except those only which they delegated to the Congress of the United States or the departments of the Federal Government.   In the language of the Tenth Amendment: "The powers not delegated to the United States by the Constitution, nor prohibited by it to the States, are reserved to the States respectively, or to the people."   Hence, as Justice Story says: "The whole power over the subject of religion is left exclusively to the State governments, to be acted upon according to their sense of justice and the State constitutions."   The States are sovereign within the limits of the supreme sovereignty of the general government, which is confined to a specified number of departments of general national interest, such as army and navy, diplomatic intercourse, post-office, coinage of money, disposal of public lands, and the government of Territories.

In New York and Virginia the union of church and state was abolished before the formation of the Federal Constitution; but in other States it continued for many years afterward, though without persecution.   Connecticut and Massachusetts retained and exercised (the former till 1818, the latter till 1833) the power of taxing the people for the support of the Congregational Church, and when such taxation was finally abolished, many good and intelligent people feared disastrous consequences for the fate of religion, but their fears were happily disappointed by the result.   In Pennsylvania, North Carolina, South Carolina, Tennessee, Maryland, and New Jersey, atheists, and such as deny "a future state of reward and punishment," are excluded from public offices, and blasphemy is subject to punishment.[1]   In Delaware, Kentucky, Maryland, and Tennessee, clergymen are not eligible for civil offices and for the legislature, on account of their ecclesiastical functions.   The constitution of New Hampshire empowers the legislature to authorize towns, parishes, and religious

[1] See the constitutional provisions of these States in Judge Cooley's "Constitutional Limitations," p. 579, note.

societies to make adequate provision, at their own expense, for the support of public *Protestant* worship, but not to tax those of other sects or denominations. An attempt was made in 1876 to amend this article by striking out the word *Protestant*, but it failed.[1]

It is remarkable, however, that since the adoption of the Federal Constitution no attempt has been made to establish a religion, except in the Mormon Territory of Utah.

Most of the more recent State constitutions expressly guarantee religious liberty to the full extent of the First Amendment, and in similar language. We give a few specimens:[1]

The constitution of Illinois (II. 3) declares that "the free exercise and enjoyment of religious profession and worship, without discrimination, shall forever be guaranteed, and no person shall be denied any civil or political right, privilege, or capacity on account of his religious opinions," and that "no person shall be required to attend or support any ministry or place of worship against his consent, nor shall any preference be given by law to any denomination or mode of worship."

The constitution of Iowa (I. 3, 4) declares that "the general assembly shall make no law respecting an establishment of religion, or prohibiting the free exercise thereof ; nor shall any person be compelled to attend any place of worship, pay tithes, taxes, or other rates for building or repairing places of worship, or the maintenance of any minister or ministry. No religious test shall be required as a qualification for any office or public trust, and no person shall be deprived of any of his rights, privileges or capacities, or disqualified from the performance of any of his public or private duties, or rendered incompetent to give evidence in any court of law or equity, in consequence of his opinion on the subject of religion."

Similar provisions are made in the constitutions of Alabama, California, Colorado, Connecticut, Florida, Georgia, Indiana, Kansas, Maryland, Michigan, Minnesota, Mississippi, Missouri, Nevada, New Jersey, New York, Oregon,

[1] Cooley, *l. c.*, p. 580, note 2.

Texas, and other States, but usually with an express caution against licentiousness and immoral practices.[1]

Judge Cooley enumerates five points which are not lawful under any of the American constitutions: 1. " Any law respecting an establishment of religion." 2. "Compulsory support, by taxation or otherwise, of religion." 3. " Compulsory attendance upon religious worship." 4. " Restraints upon the free exercise of religion according to the dictates of conscience." 5. " Restraints upon the expression of religious belief." [2]

The exceptions are remnants of older ideas, and cannot resist the force of modern progress.

It is a serious question whether the constitutions of all the States should not be so amended—if necessary—as to prevent the appropriation of public money for sectarian purposes. Such appropriations have been made occasionally by the legislature and the city government of New York in favor of the Roman Catholics, owing to the political influence of the large Irish vote. The State must, above all things, be just, and support either all or none of the religious denominations.

The case of Mormonism is altogether abnormal and irreconcilable with the genius of American institutions. In that system politics and religion are identified, and polygamy is sanctioned by religion, as in Mohammedanism. This is the reason why the Territory of Utah, notwithstanding its constitutional number of inhabitants, has not yet been admitted into the family of independent States. The general government cannot attack the religion of the Mormons, as a religion, but it can forbid polygamy as a social institution, inconsistent with our western civilization, and the Supreme Court has decided in favor of the constitutionality of such prohibition by Congress.[3] The Mormons must give up this part of their religion, or emigrate.

EFFECT OF THE CONSTITUTION UPON THE CREEDS.

The ancient or œcumenical creeds (the Apostles', the

[1] See Cooley, *l. c.*, Ch. XIII., 579 *sq.*, and especially Ben: Perley Poore. " The Federal and State Constitutions, Colonial Charters and Other Organic Laws of the United States. Compiled under an order of the U. S. Senate." Washington, 1877, two large vols.   [2] *L. c.*, p. 580.

[3] See above, p. 36, and Document II.

Nicene, and the Athanasian) are silent on the relation of church and state, and leave perfect freedom on the subject, which lies outside of the articles of faith necessary to salvation.

But some Protestant confessions of faith, framed in the Reformation period, when church and state were closely interwoven, ascribe to the civil magistrate ecclesiastical powers and duties which are Erastian or cæsaro-papal in principle and entirely inconsistent with the freedom and self-government of the church. Hence changes in the political articles of those confessions became necessary.

The Presbyterian Church took the lead in this progress even long before the American Revolution. The synod of Philadelphia, convened September 19, 1729, adopted the Westminster standards of 1647, with a liberal construction and with the express exemption of " some clauses in the XXth and XXIIId chapters of the Confession in any such sense as to imply that the civil magistrate hath a controlling power over synods with respect to the exercise of their ministerial authority or power *to persecute any for their religion*." [1]

After the revolutionary war, the United Synod of Philadelphia and New York met at Philadelphia, May 28, 1787, (at the same time and in the same place as the convention which framed the Federal Constitution), and proposed important alterations in the Westminster Confession, chapters XX. (closing paragraph), XXIII. 3, and XXXI. 1, 2, so as to eliminate the principle of state-churchism and religious persecution, and to proclaim the religious liberty and legal equality of all Christian denominations. These alterations were formally adopted by the Joint Synod at Philadelphia, May 28, 1788, and have been faithfully adhered to by the large body of the Presbyterian Church in America. It is worthy of note that the Scripture passages quoted by the old Confession in favor of state-churchism and the ecclesiastical power of the civil magistrate are all taken from the Old Testament.

The alterations may be seen from the following parallel texts:

[1] See Moore's " Presbyterian Digest," Philadelphia, second ed., 1873, p. 4 *seq.*

ORIGINAL TEXT, 1647.

Ch. XXIII. 3.—Of the Civil Magistrate.

The civil magistrate may not assume to himself the administration of the Word and Sacraments, or the power of the keys of the kingdom of heaven; [1] yet he hath authority, and it is his duty to take order, that unity and peace be preserved in the Church, that the truth of God be kept pure and entire, that all blasphemies and heresies be suppressed, all corruptions and abuses in worship and discipline prevented or reformed, and all the ordinances of God duly settled, administered, and observed. [2] For the better effecting whereof he hath power to call synods, to be present at them, and to provide that whatsoever is transacted in them be according to the mind of God. [3]

AMERICAN TEXT, 1788.

Ch. XXIII. 3.—Of the Civil Magistrate.

Civil Magistrates may not assume to themselves the administration of the Word and Sacraments, [1] or the power of the keys of the kingdom of heaven ; [2] or, in the least, interfere in matters of faith. [3] Yet, as nursing fathers, it is the duty of civil magistrates to protect the Church of our common Lord, without giving the preference to any denomination of Christians above the rest, in such a manner that all ecclesiastical persons whatever shall enjoy the full, free, and unquestioned liberty of discharging every part of their sacred functions without violence or danger. [4] And, as Jesus Christ hath appointed a regular government and discipline in his Church, no law of any commonwealth should interfere with, let, or hinder the due exercise thereof, among the voluntary members of any denomination of Christians, according to their own profession and belief. [5] It is the duty of civil magistrates to protect the person and good name of all their people, in such an effectual manner as that no person be suffered, either upon pretence of religion or infidelity, to offer any indignity, violence, abuse, or injury to any other person whatsoever ; and to take order that all religious and ecclesiastical assemblies be held without molestation or disturbance. [6]

[1] 2 Chron. xxvi. 18 ; Matt. xviii. 17 ; xvi. 19 ; 1 Cor. xii. 28, 29 ; Eph. iv. 11, 12 ; 1 Cor. iv. 1, 2 ; Rom. x. 15 ; Heb. v. 4.
[2] Isa. xlix. 23 ; Psa. cxxii. 9 ; Ezra vii. 23-28 ; Lev. xxiv. 16 ; Deut. xiii. 5, 6, 12 ; 2 Kings xviii. 4 ; 1 Chron. xiii. 1-9 ; 2 Kings xxiii. 1-26 ; 2 Chron. xv. 12, 13.
[3] 2 Chron. xix. 8-11 ; chaps. xxix. and xxx. ; Matt. ii. 4, 5.

[1] 2 Chron. xxvi. 18.
[2] Matt. xvi. 19 ; 1 Cor. iv. 1, 2.
[3] John xviii. 36. Mal. ii. 7 ; Acts v. 29.
[4] Isa. xlix. 23.
[5] Psa. cv. 15 ; Acts, xviii. 14, 15, 16.
[6] 2 Sam. xxiii. 3 ; 1 Tim. ii. 1 ; Rom. xiii. 4.

ORIGINAL TEXT, 1647.—*Continued.*

Ch. XXXI.—Of Synods and Councils.

I. For the better government and further edification of the church, there ought to be such assemblies as are commonly called synods or councils.[1]

II. As magistrates may lawfully call a synod of ministers and other fit persons to consult and advise with about matters of religion[2]; so, if magistrates be open enemies to the church, the ministers of Christ, of themselves, by virtue of their office, or they, with other fit persons, upon delegation from their churches, may meet together in such assemblies.[3]

[1] Acts xv. 2, 4, 6.
[2] Isa. xlix. 23 ; 1 Tim. ii. 1, 2 ; 2 Chron. xix. 8–11 ; chaps. xxix. and xxx. ; Matt. ii. 4, 5 ; Prov. xi. 14.
[3] Acts xv. 2, 4, 22, 23, 25.

AMERICAN TEXT, 1788.—*Continued.*

Ch. XXXI.—Of Synods and Councils.

I. For the better government and further edification of the church, there ought to be such assemblies as are commonly called synods or councils.[1]

And it belongeth to the overseers and other rulers of the particular churches, by virtue of their office, and the power which Christ hath given them for edification, and not for destruction, to appoint such assemblies ; and to convene together in them, as often as they shall judge it expedient for the good of the church.[2]

[1] Acts xv. 2, 4, 6.
[2] Acts xv. 22, 23, 25.

In Ch. XX., § 4, the last sentence, " and by the power of the civil magistrate," was omitted, so as to read, " they [the offenders] may lawfully be called to account, and proceeded against by the censures of the Church."

The only change made in the Larger Catechism was the striking out of the words " tolerating a false religion," among the sins forbidden in the Second Commandment (Quest. 109).

Two smaller Presbyterian bodies, the Associate Church, and the Reformed Presbyterian Church, adhere to the theory of the Scotch Covenanters, and abstain from voting till the Constitution is so amended as to acknowledge the sovereignty of God and the subserviency of the state to the kingdom of Christ ; but they nevertheless claim the freedom and independence of the church from the state.[1]

The example set by the Presbyterian Church in the United States was followed by the Protestant Episcopal Church, which was organized as a distinct communion in consequence of the separation from the Crown and Church of England in 1785. At first this church made radical

[1] Schaff's " Creeds of Christendom," vol. i. 811–813.

changes in her liturgy and reduced the Thirty-nine Articles to twenty, and afterward to seventeen, and omitted the Nicene and Athanasian creeds altogether under the influence of latitudinarianism which prevailed at that time.   But the " Proposed Book," or provisional liturgy of 1786, which embodied these changes, failed to give satisfaction and was opposed by the English bishops.   The General Convention at Trenton, New Jersey, September 8-12, 1801, adopted the Thirty-nine Articles, yet with the omission of the Athanasian Creed in Article VIII., and of Article XXXVII., on the Powers of the Civil Magistrate.   This article asserts in the first paragraph that

" The Queen's [King's] Majesty hath the chief power in this realm of England and other of her [his] dominions, unto whom the chief government of all estates of this realm, *whether they be ecclesiastical* or civil, in all causes doth appertain, and it is not, nor ought to be, subject to any foreign jurisdiction."

For this first section the following neccessary improvement was substituted in the American revision:

" The power of the civil magistrate extendeth to all men, as well clergy as laity, in all things temporal ; *but hath no authority in things purely spiritual.* And we hold it to be the duty of all men who are professors of the gospel, to pay respectful obedience to the civil authority, regularly and legitimately constituted."

The rest of the Article is omitted.   Article XXI., which, asserts that " General Councils may not be gathered together *without the commandment and will of princes,"* was also omitted, and Articles XXXV. (*Of the Homilies*) and XXXIX. (*Of a Christian man's Oath*) were abridged.[1]

As to the Methodists, who are the most numerous body of Protestant Christians in the United States, they had previously disowned the political articles of the Church of England by adopting the abridgment of John Wesley, who in 1784 had reduced the Thirty-nine Articles to twenty-five.[2]

The Lutheran Formula of Concord (1576) excludes the Anabaptists from toleration " in the church and in the

[1] See the texts of the Anglican and Anglo-American Articles in parallel columns in Schaff's " Creeds," vol. iii. 487-516.

[2] Schaff, iii. 807, *sqq.*

state." [1] But this prohibition has recently been legally re-moved or ceased to be enforced even in strictly Lutheran countries. In the United States it has no meaning.

The Baptists and Quakers have always protested against the union of church and state, and against all kinds of religious intolerance.

The independence of the church from the state is uni-versally adopted, and religious persecution is universally condemned, even by the most orthodox and bigoted of the American churches.

THE NATION AND CHRISTIANITY.

The separation of church and state as it exists in this country is not a separation of the nation from Christianity.

This seems paradoxical and impossible to all who entertain an absolutist or utopian idea of the state, and identify it either with the government, as did Louis XIV. (according to his maxim: *L'état c'est moi*)[2], or with the realization of the moral idea, as Hegel[3] and Rothe,[4] or with the nation, as Bluntschli,[5] and Mulford.[6]

[1] "*Anabaptistæ . . . talem doctrinam profitentur quæ neque in Ecclesia neque in politia [Germ. ed.: noch in der Polizei und weltlichem Regiment], neque in æconomia [Haushaltung] tolerari potest.*"—Epitome, Art. XII. See Schaff, *l. c.*, iii. 173.

[2] This corresponds to the Roman Catholic idea that the clergy or hierarchy are the church ; while the laity are doomed to passive obedience. Pope Pius IX. said during the Vatican Council : "I am the tradition."

[3] "Philosophie des Rechts." Hegel calls the state "*die Wirklichkeit der sittlichen Idee*," "*die selbstbewusste Vernünftigkeit und Sittlichkeit*," "*das System der sittlichen Welt.*" ("Works," vol. viii. p. 340 *sqq.*)

[4] Richard Rothe, in his "Anfänge der christlichen Kirche," (Wittenberg, 1837, pp. 1–138), teaches the ultimate absorption of religion into morals, and of the church into an ideal state, which he identifies with the kingdom of God (the βασιλεία τοῦ θεοῦ). But the ultimate state is a theocracy where God shall be all in all. (1 Cor. xv. 28.)

[5] "Lehre vom modernen Staat." Engl. translation : "Theory of the Modern State," Oxford, 1885.

[6] "The Nation : The Foundations of Civil and Political Life in the United States," Boston, 1870, 9th edition, 1884. This work grew out of the enthusiasm for the nation enkindled by the civil war for its salvation. It is a profound study of speculative politics, with the main ideas borrowed from Bluntschli, and Hegel. Mulford wrote afterwards a theological treatise under the title, "The Republic of God," Boston, 9th ed., 1886.

The tendency of modern times is to limit the powers of the government, and' to raise the liberty of the people. The government is for the people, and not the people for the government. In ancient Greece and Rome the free man was lost in the citizen, and the majority of the people were slaves. Plato carried this idea to the extent of community of property, wives, and children, in his utopian republic. Against this Aristotle protested with his strong realistic sense, and defended in his " Politics " the rights of property and the dignity of the family. The American ideal of the state is a republic of self-governing freemen who are a law to themselves. "That government is best which governs least."

The state can never be indifferent to the morals of the people ; it can never prosper without education and public virtue. Nevertheless its direct and chief concern in our country is with the political, civil, and secular affairs ; while the literary, moral, and religious interests are left to the voluntary agency of individuals, societies, and churches, under the protection of the laws. In Europe the people look to the government for taking the initiative ; in America they help themselves and go ahead.

The nation is much broader and deeper than the state, and the deepest thing in the nation's heart is its religion.

If we speak of a Christian nation we must take the word in the qualified sense of the prevailing religious sentiment and profession ; for in any nation and under any relation of church and state, there are multitudes of unbelievers, misbelievers, and hypocrites. Moreover, we must not measure the Christian character of a people by outward signs, such as crosses, crucifixes, pictures, processions, clerical coats, and monastic cowls, all of which abound in Roman Catholic countries and in Russia, on the streets and in public places, but are seldom seen in the United States. We must go to the churches and Sunday-schools, visit the houses and family altars, attend the numerous meetings of synods, conferences, conventions, observe the sacred stillness of the Lord's Day, converse with leading men of all professions and grades of culture, study the religious literature and periodical press with its accounts of the daily thoughts, words, and deeds of the people. A foreigner may at first get bewildered by the seeming confusion of ideas, and be repelled by strange novelties or eccentricities; but he will gradually be impressed with the unity and strength of the national sentiment on all vital questions of religion and morals.

With this understanding we may boldly assert that the American nation is as religious and as Christian as any nation on earth, and in some respects even more so, for the very reason that the profession and support of religion are left entirely free. State-churchism is apt to breed hypocrisy and infidelity, while free-churchism favors the growth of religion.

Alexis de Tocqueville, the most philosophic foreign observer of American institutions, says:

"There is no country in the whole world in which the Christian religion retains a greater influence over the souls of men than in America, and there can be no greater proof of its utility, and of its conformity to human nature, than that its influence is most powerfully felt over the most enlightened and free nation of the earth. . . . In the United States religion exercises but little influence upon the laws and upon the details of public opinion, but it directs the manners of the community, and by regulating domestic life, it regulates the state. . . . Religion in America takes no direct part in the government of society, but it must, nevertheless, be regarded as the foremost of the political institutions of that country, for if it does not impart a taste for freedom, it facilitates the use of free institutions. I am certain that the Americans hold religion to be indispensable to the maintenance of republican institutions. This opinion is not peculiar to a class of citizens or to a party, but it belongs to the whole nation and to every rank of society." [1]

This judgment of the celebrated French scholar and statesman is extremely important, and worthy of being seriously considered by all our educators and politicians, in opposition to infidels and anarchists, foreign and domestic, who are zealous in spreading the seed of atheism and irreligion, and are undermining the very foundations of our republic. I fully agree with De Tocqueville. I came to the same conclusion soon after my immigration to America in 1844, and I have been confirmed in it by an experience of forty-three years and a dozen visits to Europe. In Roman Catholic

[1] "Democracy in America," translated by Henry Reeve, New York, 1838, vol. i. pp. 285, 286 *sq.*

countries and in Russia there is more outward show, in Protestant countries more inward substance, of religion. There
the common people are devout and churchy, but ignorant
and superstitious ; while the educated classes are skeptical
or indifferent. In Protestant countries there is more information and intelligent faith, but also a vast amount of rationalism and unbelief. In Great Britain Christianity has a
stronger hold on all classes of society than on the Continent,
and this is partly due to the fact that it·is allowed more
freedom.

Religious Activity.

The Christian character of the American nation is apparent
from the following facts :

1. The United States equal and even surpass most Christian countries in religious energy and activity of every kind.
The rapid multiplication of churches, Sunday-schools, Young
Men's Christian Associations, religious and charitable institutions all over the country, by voluntary contributions, without any aid from the government, has no parallel in history.
Nowhere are churches better attended, the Lord's Day more
strictly observed, the Bible more revered and studied, the
clerical profession more respected, than in North America.

It is so often asserted by the advocates of state-churchism
that the clergy are made servants of the congregation from
which they draw their support. In reply we say, that they
ought to be servants of the people in the best sense of the
word, as Christ came to serve, and washed his disciples'
feet ; that American ministers are esteemed in proportion to
the fidelity and fearlessness with which they discharge their
duty to God and men ; and that the congregation feel more
attached to a pastor whom they choose and support, than to
a pastor who is set over them by the government whether he
suits them or not. A congregation is not a flock of sheep.

We may quote here a just and noble tribute which a statesman, Daniel Webster, the American Demosthenes, paid to
the American clergy, in his famous speech on the Girard
will case [1] :

[1] " Works of Daniel Webster," vol. vi. pp. 140, 141. Tenth ed., Boston, 1857.

"I take it upon myself to say, that in no country in the world, upon either continent, can there be found a body of ministers of the gospel who perform so much service to man, in such a full spirit of self-denial, under so little en- couragement from government of any kind, and under circumstances almost always much straitened and often distressed, as the ministers of the gospel in the United States, of all denominations. They form no part of any established order of religion ; they constitute no hierarchy ; they enjoy no peculiar privi- leges. In some of the States they are even shut out from all participation in the political rights and privileges enjoyed by their fellow-citizens. They enjoy no tithes, no public provision of any kind. , Except here and there, in large cities, where a wealthy individual occasionally makes a donation for the sup- port of public worship, what have they to depend upon ? They have to depend entirely on the voluntary contributions of those who hear them.

"And this body of clergymen has shown, to the honor of their own country and to the astonishment of the hierarchies of the Old World, that it is practi- cable in free governments to raise and sustain by voluntary contributions alone a body of clergymen, which, for devotedness to their sacred calling, for purity of life and character, for learning, intelligence, piety, and that wisdom which cometh from above, is inferior to none, and superior to most others.

"I hope that our learned men have done something for the honor of our literature abroad. I hope that the courts of justice and members of the bar of this country have done something to elevate the character of the profession of the law. I hope that the discussions above (in Congress) have done something to meliorate the condition of the human race, to secure and extend the great charter of human rights, and to strengthen and advance the great principles of human liberty. But I contend that no literary efforts, no adjudications, no constitutional discussions, nothing that has been done or said in favor of the great interests of universal man, has done this country more credit, at home or abroad, than the establishment of our body of clergymen, their support by voluntary contributions, and the general excellence of their character for piety and learning.

"The great truth has thus been proclaimed and proved, a truth which I believe will in time to come shake all the hierarchies of Europe, that the vol- untary support of such a ministry, under free institutions, is a practicable idea."

Christian Legislation.

2. Our laws recognize Christianity, protect church proper- ty, and decide cases of litigation according to the creed and constitution of the denomination to which the property belongs.

The Supreme Court of the United States in the case of Watson *vs.* Jones, concerning a disputed Presbyterian church property in Louisville, Kentucky, decided (Decem- ber, 1871) that:

" In such cases where the right of property in the civil court is dependent on the question of doctrine, discipline, ecclesiastical law, rule, or custom, or church government, and that has been decided by the highest tribunal within the organization to which it has been carried, *the civil court will accept that decision as conclusive, and be governed by it in its application to the case before it.*" [1]

Christianity is a part of the common law of England, according to the judicial declaration of Sir Matthew Hale and other English judges.[2] The same may be said of the United States to a limited extent, namely as far as the principles and precepts of Christianity have been incorporated in our laws, and as far as is consistent with religious and denominational equality. For our laws give no preference to any creed, but protect all alike. They protect Jews as well as Christians, infidels as well as believers, in the enjoyment of their rights, provided they do not disturb the public peace.

The Supreme Court of Pennsylvania, in the case of *Updegraph against the Commonwealth*, February sessions, 1822, argued in the Mayor's Court of the city of Pittsburg, decided that " Christianity is and always has been a part of the common law of Pennsylvania "; and that " maliciously to vilify the Christian religion is an indictable offence." [3] This Christianity was, however, defined by Judge Duncan, who delivered the opinion of the court, as " *general* Christianity, without the spiritual artillery of European countries; not Christianity founded on any particular religious tenets; not Christianity with an established church, and tithes, and spiritual courts, but *Christianity with liberty of conscience to all men.*" [4]

Daniel Webster, in the celebrated Girard will case, argued

---

[1] " United States Supreme Court Reports," 13. Wallace, p. 680. (In " Cases Argued and Adjudged, December Term, 1871.")

[2] Blackstone, " Commentaries," Book IV. 59, says : " Christianity is part of the laws of England."

[3] Abner Updegraph, of Pittsburg, was charged with vilifying the Christian religion and declaring that the Holy Scriptures were a mere fable, and contained, with a number of good things, a great many lies. See " Reports of Cases adjudged in the Supreme Court of Pennsylvania," by Thomas Sergeant and William Rawle, Jr. Phila., vol. xi. 394, *sqq.* The opinion is given in full in Document IX.

[4] *Ibid.* p. 400.

before the United States Supreme Court in Washington, February, 1844, took the same view and gave it a wider application. The most eloquent and impressive part of his argument against the will is that in which he shows the close connection of education with religion. We quote the following passage :

"It is the same in Pennsylvania as elsewhere ; the general principles and public policy are sometimes established by constitutional provisions, sometimes by legislative enactments, sometimes by judicial decisions, sometimes by general consent. But however they may be established, there is nothing that we look for with more certainty than the general principle that Christianity is part of the law of the land. This was the case among the Puritans of New England, the Episcopalians of the Southern States, the Pennsylvania Quakers, the Baptists, the mass of the followers of Whitefield and Wesley, and the Presbyterians ; all brought and all adopted this great truth, and all have sustained it. And where there is any religious sentiment amongst men at all, this sentiment incorporates itself with the law. *Every thing declares it.* The massive cathedral of the Catholic ; the Episcopalian church, with its lofty spire pointing heavenward ; the plain temple of the Quaker ; the log church of the hardy pioneer of the wilderness ; the mementos and memorials around and about us ; the consecrated graveyards, their tombstones and epitaphs, their silent vaults, their mouldering contents,—all attest it. *The dead prove it as well as the living.* The generations that are gone before speak it, and pronounce it from the tomb. We feel it. All, all proclaim that Christianity, general, tolerant Christianity, Christianity independent of sects and parties, that Christianity to which the sword and fagot are unknown, general, tolerant Christianity, is the law of the land." [1]

The Supreme Court sustained the will and the previous decision of the Circuit Court of the Eastern District of Pennsylvania (1841), but on the ground that, while it excluded *ecclesiastics* from holding office in Girard College, it was not expressly *hostile* to the Christian religion, and did not *forbid* the reading of the Bible and the teaching of unsectarian Christianity by *laymen.* Justice Story, in delivering the opinion of the court, admitted that "the Christian religion is truly a part of the common law of Pennsylvania," but that this proposition is to be received with its appropriate qualifications, and in connection with the bill of rights of that State and the full liberty of religion guaranteed by the constitution of 1790 and 1838. He concludes :

[1] Webster's " Works," vol. vi. 176.   The italics are Webster's.

" So that we are compelled to admit that, although Christianity be a part of the common law of this State, yet it is so in this qualified sense, that its divine origin and truth are admitted, and therefore it is not to be maliciously and openly reviled and blasphemed against, to the annoyance of believers or the injury of the public. Such was the doctrine of the Supreme Court of Pennsylvania in Updegraph *v.* The Commonwealth, 11 Serg. and Rawle, 394." [1]

In the State of New York Christianity is likewise recognized by the law, and blasphemy is punishable. In the case of *The people against Ruggles*, who was indicted, December, 1810, for blasphemous utterances concerning Christ, the Supreme Court at Albany, August, 1811, confirmed the judgmenh of imprisonment and a fine of $500.[2] Chief-Justice James Kent, one of the fathers of American jurisprudence, and author of the "Commentaries on American Law," in delivering the opinion of the court, declared that "we are a Christian people," and said :

" The free, equal, and undisturbed enjoyment of religious opinion, whatever it may be, and free and decent discussions on any religious subject, are granted and secured ; but to revile with malicious and blasphemous contempt the religion professed by almost the whole community is an abuse of that right. . . . We are a Christian people, and the morality of the country is deeply ingrafted upon Christianity. . . . This declaration [of the New York Constitution in favor of religious liberty] never meant to withdraw religion in general, and with it the best sanctions of moral and social obligation, from all consideration and motive of the law. To construe it as breaking down the common law barriers against licentious, wanton, and impious attacks upon Christianity itself, would be an enormous perversion of its meaning."

In the important case of *The people vs. Lindenmüller* (who had openly violated the Sunday laws and caused successive suits), the Supreme Courtof the State of New York, May 29, 1861, strongly maintained the same ground. Justice Allen in delivering the opinion, his associates concurring, said :

[1] "Reports of Cases Argued and Adjudged in the Supreme Court of the United States, January Term, 1844." By B. C. Howard. Vol. ii., Phila., 1845, p. 183 *sqq.*, especially pp. 198 and 199. The Girard College is a noble institution for the education of orphans, and has, so far, had earnest Christian laymen as presidents, who conduct it in the spirit of unsectarian Christianity.

[2] "Reports of Cases Argued and Determined in the Supreme Court of Judicature in the State of New York." By William Johnson, vol. viii. p. 290 *sqq.* See the whole decision in Document X.

" Christianity is not the legal religion of the State, as established by law. If it were, it would be a civil or political institution, which it is not ; but this is not inconsistent with the idea that *it is in fact, and ever has been, the religion of the people.* This fact is everywhere prominent in all our civil and political history, and has been, from the first, recognized and acted upon by the people, as well as by constitutional conventions, by legislatures, and by courts of justice." [1]

A similar position of the connection between Christianity and the state is taken by the courts of Massachusetts, Delaware, and New Jersey.[2]

Judge Theodore W. Dwight, president of the Columbia Law School, New York, and one of the most learned jurists in the United States, whom I consulted on the subject, gives his opinion in a letter as follows :

" It is well settled by decisions in the courts of the leading States of the Union—*e. g.*, New York, Pennsylvania, and Massachusetts—that Christianity is a part of the common law of the state. Its recognition is shown in the administration of oaths in the courts of justice, in the rules, which punish those who wilfully blaspheme, in the observance of Sunday, in the prohibition of profanity, in the legal establishment of permanent charitable trusts, and in the legal principles which control a parent in the education and training of his children. One of the American courts (that of Pennsylvania) states the law in this manner: Christianity is and always has been a part of the common law of this State— 'Christianity without the spiritual artillery of European countries—not Christianity founded on any particular religious tenets—not Christianity with an established church and tithes and spiritual courts, but Christianity with liberty of conscience to all men.'

" The American States adopted these principles from the common law of England, rejecting such portions of the English law on this subject as were not suited to their customs and institutions. Our national development has in it the best and purest elements of historic Christianity, as related to the government of States. Should we tear Christianity out of our law, we would rob our law of its fairest jewels, we would deprive it of its richest treasures, we would arrest its growth, and bereave it of its capacity to adapt itself to the progress in culture, refinement, and morality of those, for whose benefit it properly exists."

There are indeed able jurists who hold a different view, and maintain that our laws deal only with public morality.

[1] See Document XI.

[2] In New Jersey a man was recently punished for blasphemy, in spite of the eloquent defence of Colonel Robert G. Ingersoll, the apostle of American infidelity, who denounced the law as an infringement of the right of free speech. An editorial in the *Albany Law Journal*, June 4, 1887, on this case, defends the constitutionality, but doubts the policy of such prosecutions.

Nobody can be punished in this country for rejecting Christianity as a system of belief or even of conduct. But all must admit that the American system of law, whether inherited from England or enacted by statute, has grown up, together with our whole civilization, under the influence of the Christian religion, and is, directly or indirectly, indebted to it for its best elements. It breathes the spirit of justice and humanity, and protects the equal rights of all. Such a system could not have originated on heathen or Mohammedan soil. And we may say that our laws are all the more Christian because they protect the Jew and the infidel, as well as the Christian of whatever creed, in the enjoyment of the common rights of men and of citizens.

The Oath.

3. The oath, or solemn appeal to the Deity for the truth of an assertion is administered by the national government and the State governments with the use of the Bible, either in whole or in part, in conformity with old Christian custom and the national reverence for the Book of books. Simple affirmation, however, is justly allowed as a substitute,[1] in justice to the consciences of Quakers and atheists, who, from opposite motives cannot honestly take an oath. But if the affirmation proves false, it is punished as perjury. The Revised Statutes of New York provide also, that persons believing in any other than the Christian religion shall be sworn according to the peculiar ceremonies of their religion, instead of the usual mode of laying the hand upon and kissing the Gospels. Thus, a Jew may be sworn on the Old Testament, with his head covered, a Mohammedan, on the Koran, a Chinaman by breaking a china saucer. All this is simply just; and Christian, because just.

Official Acts of the Presidents.

4. Our Presidents, in their inaugural addresses, annual messages and other official documents, as well as in occasional

---

[1] It seems to have been inserted in the Federal Constitution without any debate. Madison, in the " Debates of the Federal Convention " (Elliot, v. 498) simply reports, " The words ' or affirmation,' were added after ' oath.' "

proclamations of days of thanksgiving or fasting (as during the civil war), usually recognize, more or less distinctly, the dependence of the nation upon Almighty God for all its blessings and prosperity and our duty of gratitude—at least in such general terms as a proper regard for the religion of Jewish and other citizens who reject the specific tenets of Christianity admits. Christian rulers in Europe seldom go even that far in their official utterances.

Thomas Jefferson is the only President who had constitutional scruples to appoint days of prayer and fasting, and left that to the executives of the several States. He admitted that he differed herein from his predecessors, and he would not prevent his successors from doing what is, indeed, not expressly granted, but still less forbidden by the Constitution.[1]

The father of this country, who ruled over the hearts of his fellow-citizens as completely as ever a monarch ruled over his subjects, set the example of this habitual tribute in his first and in his last official addresses to the people. In his first Inaugural Address, delivered April 30, 1789, he says :

" It would be peculiarly improper to omit, in this first official act, my fervent supplications to that Almighty Being who rules over the universe, who presides in the councils of nations, and whose providential aid can supply every human defect, that His benediction may consecrate to the liberties and happiness of the people of the United States a government instituted by themselves for these essential purposes, and may enable every instrument employed in its administration to execute with success the functions allotted to his charge. In tendering this homage to the great Author of every public and private good, I assure myself that it expresses your sentiments not less than my own ; nor those of my fellow-citizens at large, less than either. No people can be bound to acknowledge the invisible hand which conducts the affairs of men more than the people of the United States. Every step by which they have advanced to the character of an independent nation seems to have been distinguished by some token of providential agency. . . . There exists, in the economy of nature, an indissoluble union between an honest and magnanimous policy and the solid rewards of public prosperity and felicity. . . . The propitious smiles of Heaven can never smile on a nation that disregards the eternal rules of order and right which Heaven itself has ordained." [2]

[1] See his letter to Rev. Mr. Millar, in Jefferson's " Writings," vol. iv. 427, and v. 236 *sq.*

[2] " Writings of George Washington," ed. by Jared Sparks, Boston, 1837, vol. xii. 2 and 3.

And in his Farewell Address (September 7, 1796), which will never be forgotten, Washington says:

" Of all the dispositions and habits which lead to political prosperity, religion and morality are indispensable supports. For in vain would that man claim the tribute of patriotism who should labor to subvert these great pillars of human happiness, these firmest props of the duties of men and citizens. The mere politician, equally with the pious man, ought to respect and to cherish them. A volume could not trace all their connections with private and public felicity. Let it simply be asked, where is the security for property, for reputation, for life, if the sense of religious obligation desert the oaths, which are .he instruments of investigation in courts of justice ; and let us, with caution, indulge the supposition, that morality can be maintained without religion. Whatever may be conceded to the influence of refined education on minds of peculiar structure, reason and experience both forbid us to expect that national morality can prevail in exclusion of religious principle. 'T is substantially true, that virtue or morality is a necessary spring of popular government. The rule, indeed, extends with more or less force to every species of free government. Who that is a sincere friend to it can look with indifference upon attempts to shake the foundation of the fabric ? " [1]

We need not quote from the successors of Washington.[2] But we cannot omit one of the strongest official testimonies to religion from the second inaugural of President Lincoln, which is inspired by a sublime view of divine justice and mercy :

" Both [contending parties] read the same Bible and pray to the same God, and each invokes His aid against the other. It may seem strange that any men should dare to ask a just God's assistance in wringing their bread from the sweat of other men's faces, but let us judge not, that we be not judged. The prayer of both could not be answered. That of neither has been answered fully. The Almighty has His own purposes. Woe unto the world because of offences, for it must needs be that offences come, but woe to that man by whom the offence cometh. If we shall suppose that American slavery is one of these offences which, in the providence of God, must needs come, but which having continued through His appointed time, He now wills to remove, and that He gives to both North and South this terrible war as the woe due to those by whom the offence came, shall we discern there any departure from those Divine attributes which the believers in a living God always ascribe to Him ? Fondly do we hope, fervently do we pray, that this mighty scourge of war may speedily pass away. Yet if God wills that it continue until all the

---

[1] Sparks, xii. 227.

[2] Much material of this kind is, uncritically, collected by B. F. Morris, in " Christian Life and Character of Civil Institutions of the United States, developed in the Official and Historical Annals of the Republic." Philadelphia (George W. Childs), 1864. (831 pages.)

wealth piled by the bondsman's two hundred and fifty years of unrequited toil shall be sunk, and until every drop of blood drawn with the lash shall be paid by another drawn by the sword, as was said three thousand years ago, so still it must be said, that the judgments of the Lord are true and righteous altogether.

" *With malice towards none, with charity for all,* with firmness in the right as God gives us to see the right, let us finish the work we are in, to bind up the nation's wounds, to care for him who shall have borne the battle, and for his widow and his orphans, to do all which may achieve and cherish a just and a lasting peace among ourselves and with all nations." [1]

This document is without a parallel among state papers. Lincoln was of humble origin, defective education, and rugged manners, a fair type of a self-made Western American. In this second inaugural he rose above all political and diplomatic etiquette, and became, unconsciously, the prophet of the deepest religious sentiment of the nation in the darkest hour of its history. A few weeks afterwards he was assassinated, on Good Friday, April 15, 1865, and took his place next to Washington, as the martyr-president, the restorer of the Union, the emancipator of the slaves. [2]

[1] See the whole address and the stirring scene connected with the re-inauguration in Henry J. Raymond's book, " The Life and Public Services of Abraham Lincoln," New York, 1865, p. 670 *sq.*, and other biographies.

[2] Lincoln was not a communicant member of any church, though he usually attended the Presbyterian services at Springfield and Washington. But he was a deeply religious man, and rose to the highest eloquence when under the inspiration of a providential view of history, such as appears in his second inaugural. A parallel to it is his remarkable speech at the consecration of the National Soldiers' Cemetery in Gettysburg, Nov. 19, 1863, which will be read long after the formal, classical, but cold oration of Edward Everett will be forgotten. " Fourscore and seven years ago," he said, " our fathers brought forth upon this continent a new nation, conceived in liberty, and dedicated to the proposition that all men are created equal. Now, we are engaged in a great civil war, testing whether that nation, or any nation so conceived and so dedicated, can long endure. We are met on a great battle-field of that war. We have come to dedicate a portion of that field as a final resting-place for those who here gave their lives that that nation might live. It is altogether fitting and proper that we should do this. But in a larger sense we cannot dedicate, we cannot consecrate, we cannot hallow this ground. The brave men, living and dead, who struggled here, have consecrated it far above our power to add or detract. The world will little note, nor long remember, what we say here, but it can never forget what they did here. It is for us, the living, rather to be dedicated here to the unfinished work which they who fought here have thus far so nobly advanced. It is rather for us to be here dedicated

Exemption of Church Property from Taxation.

5. Our government, both Federal and State, respects the sentiment of the great majority of the people by various provisions, which are, perhaps, not strictly constitutional, though not anti-constitutional, and all the more important as voluntary tributes.

The most valuable of these provisions is the exemption of church property from taxation in the Federal District of Columbia, and in nearly all the States. In some States (Minnesota, Kansas, Arkansas) this exemption is secured by the constitution, in others by legislative enactment. No discrimination is made between different creeds and sects. Jewish synagogues are included as well as Roman cathedrals. The Revised Statutes of New York State provide that "every building for public worship" shall be exempt from taxation.

The exemption is a great help to poor churches, but by no means necessary. The people who are able and willing to spend large sums for the erection of church buildings could not plead inability to pay the small sum for the legal protection of their property. All taxation is a burden, but easier to bear for corporations than individuals.

The exemption of property used for religious purposes might be abolished without detriment to religion, but it is founded in justice and can be defended on the same ground as the exemption of government buildings, colleges, public schools, hospitals, and other charitable institutions which make no money and are intended for the benefit of the people. Besides, churches improve the morals of the surrounding community, and raise the taxable value of property.

The Appointment of Chaplains.

6. Another government tribute to the religion of the people is the appointment, at public expense, of chaplains for Con-

to the great task remaining before us, that from these honored dead we take increased devotion to that cause for which they gave the last measure of devotion ; that we here highly resolve that these dead shall not have died in vain ; that this nation, under God, shall have a new birth of freedom, and that government of the people, by the people, and for the people, shall not perish from the earth."

gress (one for the Senate and one for the House of Representatives), for the Army and Navy, and for the military
and naval academies. These chaplains are placed among
the officers of government on the same footing with other
officers. The law requires that they be regularly ordained
ministers of some religious denomination, in good standing
at the time of their appointment, and be recommended by
some authorized ecclesiastical body, or by not less than five
accredited ministers of said body. Proper facilities must be
provided by the military and naval commanders for the
holding of public worship at least once on each Sunday.
Chaplains are elected from all denominations, Roman Catholic and Protestant, according to circumstances, most frequently, perhaps, from the Episcopal Church, for the reason
that the Book of Common Prayer makes adequate provision for stated liturgical services, which fall in more easily
with military discipline than extemporary prayer.

The several States follow the precedent of the United
States, and appoint chaplains for the militia, the prisons
and penitentiaries, lunatic asylums, and other public institutions, also for the Legislature (to open the session with
prayer). They usually require these chaplains to be regularly ordained ministers of a Christian denomination. So
does New York, in the act providing for enrolment of
the militia, passed April 23, 1862. The prisons are provided
with a Bible in each room.

This custom also may be sufficiently justified by the
necessity of discipline and the requirement of public decorum.

Congress and the Bible.

7. We may add, as exceptional instances of favor, the
patronage extended by the Continental Congress and the
United States Congress to the authorized Protestant version and revision of the Sacred Scriptures.

In England, the printing of the authorized version of the
Scriptures (without comments) is to this day a monopoly of
the university presses of Oxford and Cambridge (which, it
must be admitted, issue the work in the best possible man-

ner, in all sizes and at all prices). No edition of the English Bible was printed in America during the entire colonial period of more than a hundred and fifty years.[1] The only Bible which appeared before the Revolution was John Eliot's Indian version (Cambridge, Massachusetts, 1661-1663), and Luther's German version (by Christopher Saur, Germantown, Pennsylvania, 1743, '63, '76).

During the revolutionary war, Bibles became so scarce that Congress was petitioned to publish the book. This was declined, but authority was given to import 20,000 copies from Europe. The first English Bible appeared in Philadelphia, 1782 (Robert Aitken). Congress submitted it to an examination by the two chaplains, Rev. W. White and George Duffield, and then recommended it "to the inhabitants of the United States," and authorized the printer "to publish this recommendation in the manner he shall think proper." This act was passed Sept. 12, 1782.

The favorable legislation of Congress in behalf of the revised version was brought about by the exertions of Colonel Elliott F. Shepard, a member of the Finance Committee of laymen aiding the American Committee on Revision. It saved them several thousand dollars by exempting from the customary duty of twenty-five per cent. as many memorial presentation volumes as they had promised to their patrons for contributions towards the expenses. This Joint Resolution of Congress was approved March 11, 1882.[2]

It is doubtful whether any European government would pass such an act in favor of the Holy Scriptures. Certainly no Roman Catholic government would do it. These acts of Congress show that the dominant form of American Christianity is Protestant. It has been so from the first settlements, is still, and is likely to abide. The fortunes of Protestantism are inseparably connected with the Bible, and the Bible has lived long enough to justify the belief that it will last as long as the world.

[1] An edition of the English Bible was advertised at Philadelphia Jan. 14, 1688, by William Bradford, but it never appeared, probably because the English copyright was in the way. [2] See Document IV.

THE CONNECTING LINKS BETWEEN CHURCH AND STATE.

A total separation of church and state is an impossibility, unless we cease to be a Christian people.

There are three interests and institutions which belong to both church and state, and must be maintained and regulated by both. These are monogamy in marriage, the weekly day of rest, and the public school. Here the American government and national sentiment have so far decidedly protected the principles and institutions of Christianity as essential elements in our conception of civilized society.

Marriage.

Monogamy, according to the unanimous sentiment of all Christian nations, is the only normal and legitimate form of marriage. It has been maintained by Congress, with the approval of the nation, in its prohibitory legislation against the new Mohammedanism in Utah, and the Supreme Court of the United States, the highest tribunal of our laws, has sanctioned the prohibition of polygamy as constitutional. The Mormons have to submit, or to emigrate to more congenial climes.

All the States uphold monogamy and punish bigamy. But some of them, unfortunately, are very loose on the subject of divorce, and a reform of legislation in conformity to the law of Christ is highly necessary for the safety and prosperity of the family. It is to the honor of the Roman Catholic Church in our country that she upholds the sanctity of the marriage tie.

Sunday Laws.

The Christian Sabbath or weekly day of rest is likewise protected by legislation, and justly so, because it has a civil as well as a religious side ; it is necessary and profitable for the body as well as for the soul ; it is of special benefit to the laboring classes, and guards them against the tyranny of capital. The Sabbath, like the family, antedates the Mosaic legislation, and is founded in the original constitution of man, for. whose temporal and spiritual benefit it was instituted by the God of creation. The state has nothing to do with the religious aspect of Sunday, but is deeply interested in its civil aspect, which affects the whole domestic and social life of a people.

The Federal Constitution, in deference to the national sentiment, incidentally recognizes Sunday by the clause (Art. I., Sect. 7): "If any bill shall not be returned by the President within ten days (*Sundays excepted*) after it shall have been presented to him, the same shall be a law in like manner as if he had signed it." Congress never meets on Sunday, except of necessity, at the close of the short term, to complete legislation if the third of March happens to fall on a Sunday. The President is never inaugurated on a Sunday. The Supreme Court and the Federal Courts are closed on that day. And if the Fourth of July falls on a Sunday, the great national festival is put off till Monday. The Revised Statutes of the United States sustain the observance of Sunday in four particulars. They exempt the cadets at West Point and the students of the Naval Academy from study on Sunday; they exclude Sunday, like the Fourth of July and Christmas Day, from computation in certain bankruptcy proceedings; and provide that army chaplains shall hold religious services at least once on each Lord's Day.

During the civil war, when the Sunday rest was very much interrupted by the army movements, the President of the United States issued the following important order:

"EXECUTIVE MANSION, WASHINGTON, Nov. 15, 1862.

"The President, Commander-in-Chief of the Army and Navy, desires and enjoins the orderly observance of the Sabbath by the officers and men in the military and naval service. The importance, for man and beast, of the prescribed weekly rest, the sacred rights of a Christian people, and a due regard for the Divine will, demand that Sunday labor in the army and navy be reduced to the measure of strict necessity. The discipline and character of the national forces should not suffer, nor the cause they defend be imperilled, by the profanation of the day or name of the Most High. At this time of public distress, adopting the words of Washington, in 1776, 'men may find enough to do in the service of God and their country, without abandoning themselves to vice and immorality.' The first general order issued by the Father of his Country, after the Declaration of Independence, indicates the spirit in which our institutions were founded and should ever be defended:

" ' The General hopes and trusts that every officer and man will endeavor to live and act as becomes a Christian soldier, defending the dearest rights and liberties of his country.'   ABRAHAM LINCOLN.'

The State legislatures, State courts, and State elections follow the example of the general government, or rather preceded it. The States are older than the United States, and Sunday is older than both.

Most of the States protect Sunday by special statutes.

These Sunday laws of the States are not positive and coercive, but negative, defensive, and protective, and as such perfectly constitutional, whatever Sabbath-breaking infidels may say. The state, indeed, has no right to command the religious observance of Sunday, or to punish anybody for not going to church, as was done formerly in some countries of Europe. Such coercive legislation would be unconstitutional and contrary to religious liberty. The private observance and private non-observance is left perfectly free to everybody. But the state is in duty bound to protect the religious community in their right to enjoy the rest of that day, and should forbid such *public* desecration as interferes with this right.

The Supreme Court of the State of New York, February 4, 1861, decided that the regulation of the Christian Sabbath "as a civil and political institution" is "within the just powers of the civil government," and that the prohibition of theatrical and dramatic performances on that day, "rests on the same foundation as a multitude of other laws on our statute-book, such as those against gambling, lotteries, keeping disorderly houses, polygamy, horse-racing, profane cursing and swearing, disturbances of religious meetings, selling of intoxicating liquor on election days within a given distance from the polls, etc. All these and many others do, to some extent, restrain the citizen and deprive him of some of his natural rights; but the legislature have the right to prohibit acts injurious to the public and subversive of government, or which tend to the destruction of the morals of the people, and disturb the peace and good order of society. It is exclusively for the legislature to determine what acts should be prohibited as dangerous to the community."[1]

[1] See the whole decision in Document XI.

The Penal Code of New York, as amended in 1882 and 1883, forbids "all labor on Sunday, excepting works of necessity or charity," and declares "Sabbath-breaking a misdemeanor, punishable by a fine of not less than one dollar and not more than ten dollars, or by imprisonment in a jail not exceeding five days, or by both." Among things expressly prohibited on Sunday, the Penal Code mentions, "all shooting, hunting, fishing, playing, horse-racing, gaming, or other public sports, exercises, or shows"; "all trades, manufactures, agricultural or mechanical employments"; "all manner of public selling or offering for sale of any property" (except articles of food and meals); "all service of legal process of any kind whatever"; "all processions and parades" (except funeral processions and religious processions); "the performance of any tragedy, comedy, opera," or any other dramatic performance (which is subjected to an additional penalty of five hundred dollars).[1]

The opposition to the Sunday laws comes especially from the foreign population, who have grown up under the demoralizing influence of the continental Sunday, and are not yet sufficiently naturalized to appreciate the habits of the land of their adoption. But the more earnest and religious portion of German immigrants are in hearty sympathy with the quiet and order of the American Sunday and have repeatedly expressed it in public meetings in New York and other large cities.[2]

The only class of American citizens who might with justice complain of our Sunday laws and ask protection of the last day of the week instead of the first, are the Jews and the

[1] See "The Penal Code of New York," Title x. ch. 1, Of Crimes against Religious Liberty and Conscience.

[2] See documents of the New York Sabbath Committee, Nos. xv., xvi., xxvi., xxvii., and the author's essays on the Christian Sabbath, in "Christ and Christianity," New York and London, 1885, pp. 213–275. The most recent German demonstration in protection of the Sunday and Excise laws took place November 1, 1887, at a mass meeting in Cooper Institute, New York, against the "Personal Liberty Party," which would claim the half of Sunday from 2 P.M. till midnight for the special benefit of the liquor trade, while all other trades are prohibited. All the speeches were made in the German language and met with enthusiastic applause.

Seventh Day Baptists. But they are a small minority, and must submit to the will of the majority, as the government cannot wisely appoint two weekly days of rest. The Revised Statutes of New York, however, provide that those who keep "the last day of the week, called Saturday, as holy time, and do not labor or work on that day," shall be exempted from the penalties of the statute against labor on Sunday, provided only that their labor do not "interrupt or disturb other persons in observing the first day of the week as holy time." The law of New York exempts also the same persons from military duty and jury duty on Saturday.

The United States present, in respect to Sunday legislation and Sunday observance, a most striking contrast to the Continent of Europe, both Protestant and Roman Catholic, where Sunday is perverted from a holy day of rest and worship into a frivolous holiday of amusement and dissipation, dedicated to beer gardens, theatres, horse-races, and political elections. Judged by the standard of Sunday observance, America is the most Christian country in the world, with the only exceptions of England and Scotland.

Religion in Public Schools.

The relation of state education to religion is a most important and most difficult problem, which will agitate the country for a long time. It is increased by a difference of views within the religious denominations themselves; while on the questions of monogamy and Sunday they are substantially agreed.

The Roman Catholics, under the dictation of the Vatican, oppose our public schools, which are supported by general taxation, for the reason that *their* religion is not taught there, and that a "godless" education is worse than none. They are right in the supreme estimate of religion as a factor in education, but they are radically wrong in identifying the Christian religion with the Roman creed, and very unjust in calling our public schools "godless." They must learn to appreciate Protestant Christianity, which has built up this country and made it great, prosperous, and free. Their

Church enjoys greater liberty in the United States than in Italy or Spain or Austria or France or Mexico, and for this they should at least be grateful. They will never succeed in overthrowing the public school system, nor in securing a division of the school funds for sectarian purposes. They have a remedy in private and parochial schools, which they can multiply without let or hindrance. There is no compulsory attendance on public schools in any of our States. The only point of reasonable complaint from Catholics is that they are taxed for the support of public schools which they condemn. Strict justice would exempt them from the school tax. But the principal tax-payers are wealthy Protestants, who, for various reasons, prefer to educate their children in private schools at their own expense. The right of minorities should be protected by all means save the destruction of the rights of the majority, which must rule in a republican country. The Roman Catholics would act more wisely and patriotically by uniting with the religious portion of the Protestant community in every effort to improve the moral character of the public schools. They may be sure of a cordial disposition to meet them in every just and reasonable demand. Protestants are just as much concerned for the religious and moral training of their children as they.

The public school is and ever will be an American institution from the Atlantic to the Pacific. It dates from early colonial days in New England, and has always been, next to the church, the chief nursery of popular intelligence, virtue, and piety. The Continental Congress, in the ordinance of 1787 (Article III.), enjoined it upon the territory northwest of the Ohio River, that "schools and the means of education shall forever be encouraged," because "religion, morality, and knowledge are necessary to good government and the happiness of mankind." The public school system grows and aims higher every year. It is not satisfied with elementary instruction, but aims at a full college and university education, at least in the West, where large landed endowments come to its aid. The state has the right and the duty to educate its citizens for useful citizenship, and should give the poorest and humblest the benefit of a sufficient training for that purpose. A democratic republic based upon universal suffrage depends for its safety and prosperity upon the intelligence and virtue of the people. But virtue is based on religion, and the obligations of man to man rest upon the obligations of man to his Maker and Preserver. Intellectual training without moral training is dangerous, and moral training without religion lacks the strongest incentive which appeals to the highest motives, and quickens and energizes all the lower motives. Who can measure the influence of the single idea of an omniscient and omnipresent God who reads our thoughts afar off and who will judge all our deeds? The example of Christ is a more effectual teacher and reformer than all the moral philosophies, ancient and modern.

The state recognizes the importance of religion by allowing the reading of the Bible, the singing of a hymn, and the recital of the Lord's Prayer, or some other prayer, as opening exercises of the school. I am informed by competent authority that at least four fifths of the public schools in the United States observe this custom.[1] Most of the school teachers, especially the ladies, are members of evangelical churches, and commend religion by their spirit and example. To call such schools "godless" is simply a slander.

Some schools exclude the Bible to please the Roman Catholics, who oppose every *Protestant* version, and the Jews and infidels who oppose Christianity in any form. Other schools have found it necessary to reintroduce religious exercises for the maintenance of proper discipline.

---

[1] E. E. White, LL.D., Superintendent of Public Schools in Cincinnati, in his paper read before the National Educational Association in Topeka, Kansas, July 15, 1886, says (p. 10) : " The great majority of American schools are religious without being sectarian ; and it is high time that this fact were more universally recognized. It is doubtless true that the most impressive forms of presenting religious sanctions to the mind and heart of the young are prayer, silent or spoken, and the reverent reading of the Bible, especially those portions that present human duty in its relations to the Divine Will— forms still permitted and widely used in four fifths of the American schools "

The Catholics certainly have a right to demand the Douay version as a substitute for that of King James, and both might be read, the one to the Catholic, the other to the Protestant pupils; but they are at heart opposed to the free and independent atmosphere of thought which prevails in the schools of a Protestant community, and which is dangerous to the principles of authority and absolute obedience to the priesthood. It is vain, therefore, to expect to satisfy them by the exclusion of the Bible from the public school, which is advocated by many Protestants as a peace measure. It is better to hold on to the time-honored custom of holding up before the rising generation day by day a short and suitable lesson from the Book of books, no matter in what version. The Psalms contain the sublimest lyrical poetry; the Lord's Prayer is the best of all prayers: the Sermon on the Mount is more popular and beautiful than any moral essay; and the thirteenth chapter of First Corinthians is the most effective sermon on charity. A competent committee of clergymen and laymen of all denominations could make a judicious selection which would satisfy every reasonable demand. With unreason even the gods fight in vain.

The reading of brief Bible lessons, with prayer and singing, is a devotional exercise rather than religious instruction, but it is all that can be expected from the state, which dare not intermeddle with the differences of belief. Positive religious instruction is the duty of the family, and the church, which has the commission to teach all nations the way of life. The state cannot be safely intrusted with this duty. It might teach rationalism, as is actually done in many public schools and universities of Germany, Holland, and Switzerland.

But the state may allow the different denominations to monopolize certain school hours in the school building for religious instruction. In this way the problem of united secular and separate religious education could be solved, at least to the reasonable satisfaction of the great majority. Possibly the more liberal portion of our Roman Catholic fellow-citizens might agree to such a compromise. In communities which are sufficiently homogeneous, one teacher would answer ; in others, two or more might be chosen, and the children divided into classes according to the will of the parents or guardians.

The state is undoubtedly competent to give instruction in all elementary and secular or neutral branches of learning, such as reading and writing, mathematics, languages, geography, chemistry, natural science, logic, rhetoric, medicine, law, etc. The difficulty begins in history and the moral sciences which deal with character, touch upon religious ground, and enjoin the eternal principles of duty. A history which would ignore God, Christ, the Bible, the Church, the Reformation, and the faith of the first settlers of this country, would be nothing but a ghastly skeleton of dry bones. An education which ignores the greatest characters and events and the most sacred interests in human life must breed religious indifference, infidelity, and immorality.

But the people will not allow this as long as they remain religious and Christian. Parents will not send their children to godless schools. They have the power in their own hands ; they appoint the school boards, and through them the teachers. This is a government " of the people, by the people, and for the people." Republican institutions are a blessing or a curse according to the character of those who administer them. And so it is with our public schools. All depends at last upon competent and faithful teachers. If the teachers fear God and love righteousness, they will inspire their pupils with the same spirit ; if they do not, they will raise an infidel generation, notwithstanding the reading of the Bible and the teaching of the Catechism. It is in the interest of the educational institutions of the several States, and indispensable to their well-being, that they should maintain a friendly relation to the churches and the Christian religion, which is the best educator and civilizer of any people.

Whatever defects there are in our public schools, they can be supplied by the Sunday-schools, which are multiplying and increasing in importance with the growth of the country ; by catechetical instruction of the pastor, which ought to be revived as a special preparation for church membership ; and by private schools, academies, and denominational colleges and universities.   The church is perfectly free and untrammelled in the vast work of education, and this is all she can expect.   If she does her full duty, America will soon surpass every other country in general intelligence, knowledge, and culture.   Here is an opportunity for every man to become a gentleman, for every woman to become a lady, and for all to become good Christians.   This is the ideal, but when will it be realized?

EFFECTS OF SEPARATION OF CHURCH AND STATE.

Whatever may be the merits of the theory of the American system, it has worked well in practice.   It has stood the test of experience.   It has the advantages of the union of church and state without its disadvantages.   It secures all the rights of the church without the sacrifice of liberty and independence, which are worth more than endowments. Not that endowments are to be despised, or are inconsistent with a free church.   They are rapidly increasing in America by more than princely donations and the rise of real estate.   Literary and theological institutions ought to be liberally endowed, and every congregation ought to have a church building and a parsonage free of debt.   The Trinity Episcopal Church, and the Collegiate Reformed Dutch Church, both of New York City, are enabled by their enormous wealth to aid many charities and missions.   Yet experience teaches that endowed churches are generally less liberal than churches which depend upon the constant flow of voluntary contributions.

The necessary consequence of the separation of church and state is the voluntary principle of self-support and self-government.   Christianity is thrown upon its own resources. It has abundantly shown its ability to maintain itself without the secular arm of the government.   It did so even during the first three centuries under a hostile and persecuting government, when every congregation was a benevolent society, and provided for the poor, the sick, the stranger, and the prisoner, to the astonishment of the heathen.

1. The voluntary system develops individual activity and liberality in the support of religion ; while the state-church system has the opposite tendency. Where the treasure is, says Christ, there is the heart also. Liberality, like every virtue, grows with exercise and gradually becomes a second nature. The state gives to the church as little as possible, and has always more money for the army and navy than for religion and education.

In large cities on the Continent there are parishes of fifty thousand souls with a single pastor ; while in the United States there is on an average one pastor to every thousand members. It seems incredible that Berlin, the metropolis of the German Empire and of Protestant theology, should in 1887 have no more than about sixty church edifices for a population of twelve hundred thousand ; while the city of New York counts five times as many churches for the same number of population, and in connection with them over four hundred Sunday-schools.[1] No wonder that only about two per cent. of the inhabitants of Berlin are said to attend church, though nearly all are baptized and confirmed. And yet there are as good Christians in that city, from the highest to the lowest classes, as anywhere in the world.

The Free churches in Switzerland and Scotland and the Dissenting churches in England teach the same lesson, and by their liberality put the established churches to shame.

The progress of the United States is the marvel of modern history, in religion, no less than in population, commerce, wealth, and general civilization. Though not much older than a century, they have in this year 1887, with a popula-

[1] From "Trow's New York City Directory" for 1887 we learn that the number of churches and chapels in New York is 431. This aggregate does not include the Sunday-schools and small missions in all sections of the city. Among these churches 74 are Protestant Episcopal, 66 Roman Catholic, 66 Methodist Episcopal, 59 Presbyterian, 41 Baptist, 23 Dutch Reformed, 7 Congregational, 20 Lutheran, 32 Synagogues, and 43 of other bodies, of small size or of independent character.

tion of about sixty millions, no less than 132,434 churches or congregations, 91,911 ministers of the gospel, and 19,018,917 communicants. Church property, on an average, has doubled every decade; it amounted in 1870 to $354,483,581, and if it goes on increasing at the same rate, it will reach in 1900 the sum of nearly three billions. The number of theological schools exceeds one hundred and fifty, and a few of them are not far behind the theological faculties of the twenty-two universities of Germany.

The enormous immigration must, of course, be taken into account in the growth of the country ; but the modern immigration is not prompted by religious motives, as was the immigration in the colonial period, and contributes less to our religious progress, than to our religious destitution. Even the better class of immigrants, with many noble exceptions, are behind the native Americans in the support of religion, not from fault of nature or disposition, but from want of practice and from the bad effects of the state-church system of providing,[1] under which they have been brought up.

2. The necessity of self-support of the church at home does not diminish but increase the active zeal for the spread of the gospel abroad. Liberality in one direction creates liberality in every other direction. Those who give most for one good cause, generally give most for other good causes.

All foreign missionary operations of Christendom rest on the voluntary principle. A state-church, as such, has no interest and care for religion beyond its geographical boundaries, and leaves the conversion of the heathen to voluntary societies. Free churches, if they have the proper spirit, carry on missions in their corporate capacity, and expect every congregation and member to contribute according to ability. Each denomination has its own foreign and domestic missionary society. There are flourishing American missions in India, China, Japan, South Africa, Syria, Turkey, and the new settlements of the West are supplied with ministers from the East. In Europe the missionaries have to be trained in special institutions (as at Basel, Barmen,

[1] The *staatskirchliche Versorgungssystem*, as the Germans would call it.

Berlin), as the universities furnish very few missionaries; while the theological seminaries of the United States send annually a number of their best graduates to destitute fields at home and abroad.

3. The voluntary system develops the self-governing power of the church in the laity, and trains elders, deacons, church wardens, treasurers, debaters, and all sorts of helpers in the government and administration of ecclesiastical affairs. In state-churches the laity are passive, except as far as they are engaged in missionary, charitable, and other voluntary societies and enterprises.

4. The free-church system secures the exercise of church discipline, which is almost impossible in state-churches, and provides a purer and more efficient ministry. In state-churches the study of theology is pursued like any other profession, and the state looks only at theoretical qualifications. Teachers of theology in continental universities are appointed by the government for the promotion of theology as a science, without regard to orthodoxy and religious character, unless the minister of public worship and instruction or the sovereign happens to be concerned for these qualifications. A professor may reject or doubt half of the canon of the Bible, deny its inspiration, the holy Trinity, the divinity of Christ and the Holy Spirit, without losing his place. The church may protest, but her protest is in vain. In America, where the church appoints and supports her own officers, such anomalies are impossible, or, at all events, only exceptional. No one is expected to enter the ministry or to teach theology who is not prompted by high spiritual motives, and in cordial sympathy with the creed of his denomination. Hence the Protestant churches in America are more orthodox and active than in Europe. Theology, as a science, is not cultivated to such an extent as in Germany, but it moves more in harmony with the practical life and wants of the churches; every lecture is opened with prayer, and the day closes with devotional exercises of the professors and students.

5. The inevitable division of the Church into an indefinite

number of denominations and sects is made the strongest
objection to the free-church system by the advocates of
ecclesiastical establishments.   But free separation is more
honest than forced union.   Nearly all our divisions are inherited from Europe; the only difference is that there they
exist in the form of sects and parties, here on a basis of legal
equality.   In England there are fully as many denominations as here.[1]   The leading denominations of the United
States can be reduced to seven families, the rest are subor-
dinate branches.   If church and state were separated on the
Continent, the theological schools which now antagonize each
other under the same state-church roof would organize
themselves into separate denominations.

The tendency to division and split is inherent in Protestantism, and it must be allowed free scope until every legitimate type of Christianity is developed and matured.   The
work of history is not in vain.   But division is only a means
to a higher unity than the world has yet seen.   The ma-
jestic and rock-built cathedral of the papacy represents authority without freedom, and unity without variety.   True
unity must rest on liberty and include the greatest variety.
There is more real union and friendship between the different
denominations in America than there is between the different
theological schools and parties in the state-churches of
Europe.   The dangers of liberty are great, but no greater than
the dangers of authority, which may lead to grinding and de-
grading despotism.   America has cast her lot with the cause
of freedom, and must sink or swim, perish or survive with it.
The progress of history is a progress of freedom.   Let us
stand fast in the freedom wherewith Christ has made us
free. (Gal. v., 1.)   We must believe in the Holy Spirit, the
author and giver of life, who will never forsake the church,
but lead her higher and higher even unto perfection.

[1] Or even more, if we are to credit " The Statesman's Year-Book for 1887"
(London, 1887), which says (p. 218) : " There are altogether 180 religious denominations in Great Britain, the names of which have been given in to the
Registrar-General of Births, Deaths, and Marriages." This incredible number must include all sorts of societies which no sensible man would call a
church or a sect.

God has great surprises in store. The Reformation is not by any means the last word He has spoken. We may confidently look and hope for something better than Romanism and Protestantism. And free America, where all the churches are commingling and rivalling with each other, may become the chief theatre of such a reunion of Christendom as will preserve every truly Christian and valuable element in the various types which it has assumed in the course of ages, and make them more effective than they were in their separation and antagonism. The denominational discords will be solved at last in the concord of Christ, the Lord and Saviour of all that love, worship, and follow Him. There is no room for fear and discouragement under the banner of the Cross which still bears the device: *Τούτῳ νίκα.*[1]

RELIGIOUS LIBERTY IN MODERN EUROPE.

In conclusion we must briefly survey the influence of the American system upon foreign countries and churches.

Within the present generation the principle of religious liberty and equality, with a corresponding relaxation of the bond of union of church and state, has made steady and irresistible progress among the leading nations of Europe, and has been embodied more or less clearly in written constitutions. The French revolution of 1830, the more extensive revolutions of 1848, and the great events of 1866 and 1870 have broken down the bulwarks of intolerance, and prepared the way for constitutional changes.

The successful working of the principle of religious freedom in the United States has stimulated this progress without any official interference. All advocates of the voluntary principle and of a separation of church and state in Europe point to the example of this country as their strongest practical argument.

The separation of church and state is a far more difficult task in Europe than it was in America. There the union of the two powers is interwoven with the history of the past and with every fibre of national life. It has still great advan-

---

[1] *Hoc signo vince.*

tages: it secures an orderly administration, and a comfortable support to the clergy; it gives the church access to the whole population and brings all the young under religious instruction. In most countries of Europe, Catholic as well as Protestant, the state has secularized the landed and other possessions of the church, and in supporting the clergy, it only pays the interest of a debt assumed. The state is not likely to surrender the church property, and to lose its power over the clergy by making it independent; while the clergy is not disposed to give up its claim and to entrust itself to the good-will of the congregations for its daily bread. The United States never possessed any church property, and never meddled with ecclesiastical affairs except to protect them by law.

Nevertheless the basis on which the union of church and state is founded, namely the identity of the community of citizens and the community of Christians of one creed, no longer exists, and acts of uniformity in religion have become an impossibility. The state has sacred obligations to all its citizens, and dare not promote a creed at the expense of justice and humanity. The mixed character of the population as regards their religious convictions peremptorily demands concessions to dissenters, and every such concession or act of toleration is a weakening of the bond of union between church and state, until at last a separation becomes inevitable. This at least is the tendency of things in modern Europe. There are few intelligent advocates of state-churchism, at least in Protestant countries, who will not concede the necessity of toleration as a simple act of justice, or even go further and admit the principle of free-churchism, namely that the profession of religion ought to be voluntary, and that the church ought to support and to govern herself. The internal controversies of Christendom should be fought out on the basis of freedom without fear and favor of the secular power.

Great Britain.

England is the mother of the United States, though she acted more like a step-mother in colonial days. Our language, laws, customs, and religion, and our conception of liberty and self-government, are derived from her. Without the Magna Charta, the Petition of Right, and the Bill of Rights—the three documents which Lord Chatham called the Bible of the English Constitution,—there would be no American Constitution, which embodies their most valuable guarantees of personal and national freedom.[1]

The era of religious uniformity and consequent persecution, which sent so many of England's best citizens to the wild woods of North America, closed with the expulsion of the tyrannical and treacherous dynasty of the Stuarts and the Act of Toleration of 1689. The benefit of this act was subsequently enlarged, and extended to Unitarians (1813), to Roman Catholics (1829), and at last to the Jews (1858), all of whom may now be represented in Parliament. Practically there is as much civil and religious liberty and as much religious activity in England and Scotland as in the United States, and the voluntary principle, owing in part to the good example set by dissenters, has made wonderful progress within the established church itself.

But nominally and legally the Queen is still the supreme governor, both of the Episcopalian Church of England, and of the Presbyterian Church of Scotland; and as Empress of India she is bound to protect the Hindoo religion of her subjects. Presbyterians are dissenters in England; while Episcopalians are dissenters in Scotland. The Queen changes her churchmanship and dissentership twice every year, as she passes from Windsor to Balmoral and back again   This

---

[1] Francis Lieber ("On Civil Liberty and Self-Government," p. 260) says : "American liberty belongs to the great division of Anglican liberty [as distinguished from Gallican liberty]. It is founded upon the checks, guarantees, and self-government of the Anglican race. The trial by jury, the representative government, the common law, self-taxation, the supremacy of the law, publicity, the submission of the army to the legislature . . . form part and parcel of our liberty. There are, however, features and guarantees which are peculiar to ourselves, and which, therefore, we may say constitute American liberty. They may be summed up, perhaps, under these heads : Republican federalism, strict separation of the state from the church, greater equality and acknowledgment of abstract rights in the citizen, and a more popular or democratic cast of the whole polity."

double headship—leaving out the sex—is a strange anomaly, and without a shadow of precedent in the Bible or antiquity. It dates from Henry VIII. and Queen Elizabeth. It cannot last much longer. The dissenters are uneasy and discontented with their status of legal and social inferiority, and a large class of Episcopalians feel equally discontented with the subserviency of their own church to the royal supremacy and to a Parliament composed no more exclusively of churchmen, but also of dissenters, Jews, and Gentiles. In England and Wales the dissenters numbered in 1883 nearly one half of the population (12,500,000 to 13,500,000 Episcopalians), and in Scotland, the Free Church and United Presbyterian Church, even without the non-Presbyterian communions, are nearly as strong as the established Kirk.

In Ireland the Church of England was disestablished in 1869 under the leadership of a high-church Episcopalian prime minister, who in his youth had written an elaborate defence of the union of church and state.[1] Mr. Gladstone has not changed his religion, but he has changed his politics. After years of practical experience in government, he found it impossible to maintain his views in the mixed character of the modern state, without doing injustice to a large portion of the people. At the union of England and Ireland in 1801, it was enacted that the Churches of England and Ireland were forever to form one Protestant Episcopalian Church; and this was to be a fundamental part of the union between the two countries. The Irish were forced to support a religion which was professed only by a small minority, and which was hated as heretical and tyrannical by three fourths of the population.

---

[1] William Ewart Gladstone : " The State in its Relations with the Church." 4th ed. London, 1841. 2 vols. The famous critique of Macaulay in the " Edinburgh Review " for April, 1839, is very respectful to the author, but very severe on his theory, which, he says, ought to be built on " buttresses of adamant," but is " made out of flimsy materials fit only for perorations." For a more recent defence and exposition of Anglican state-churchism, see Roundell, Earl of Selborne : " A Defence of the Church of England against Disestablishment " (London, 1886) ; also Hon. Arthur Elliot : " The State and the Church " (London, 1882).

The wonder is, that such an anomaly could continue so long and be defended by good men misguided by hereditary prejudice. The disestablishment and disendowment of the Anglican Church in Ireland, accompanied by proper compensation or commutation, was an act of simple justice, and has resulted in giving greater efficiency to the Episcopal and other Protestant bodies.

Since that time all Christian denominations in Ireland are placed on a footing of legal equality, and each manages its affairs independently in its own way. This state of things would have appeared impossible not only to Englishmen before the Reformation, when all citizens were Roman Catholics, but also to Protestant Englishmen during the times when the principle of uniformity in religion prevailed. Now this principle is universally abandoned as oppressive, unjust, and unreasonable.

Whether disestablishment will follow in Scotland, Wales, and at last even in England, is only a question of time. True religion in these countries will be the gainer. The Free Church of Scotland started with the establishment principle, but has abandoned it under the influence of successful experience.

Switzerland.

Switzerland approaches nearest the United States in her republican organization, though differing in nationality and language. She is the oldest republic in Europe, dating from "the eternal covenant" of Uri, Schwyz, and Unterwalden, which was concluded August 1, 1291.[1]

[1] See Dr. Bluntschli (a native of Zürich, Professor of Legal Science at Heidelberg, d. 1881) : " Geschichte des Schweizerischen Bundesrechtes von den ersten ewigen Bünden bis auf die Gegenwart," 2d ed. Stuttgart, 1875. 2 vols. The second volume contains the documents. The first covenant of 1291 is in Latin, and begins : " *In nomine Domini. Amen.*" This form is followed in the later covenants. The sacred oath of the men in Grütli, on the Lake of the Four Cantons, in 1308, was a renewal of the covenant of 1291, and followed by the expulsion of the foreign rulers appointed by King Albrecht of Austria. On Dec. 9, 1315, after the memorable battle of Morgarten, the covenant was again renewed at Brunnen. The story of William Tell, immortalized by the historic skill of Johann von Müller, and still more by the poetic genius of Schiller, is unfortunately a myth, though with a kernel of truth " *Auch die Geschichte*

Originally the Swiss republic was a loose, aristocratic confederacy of independent cantons, and recognized only one religion, the Roman Catholic, in the middle ages, and two after the Reformation, the Roman Catholic and the Reformed (*i. e.*, the church reformed by Zwingli and Calvin). In 1848, after the defeat of the *Sonderbund* of the Roman Catholic cantons, which obstructed all progress, the constitution was entirely remodelled on democratic principles, and after the American example. The confederacy of cantons was changed into a federal state with a representation of the people, and with a central government acting directly upon the people. The legislative branch of the government (*Bundesversammlung*, Congress) was divided into two houses, —the *Ständerath*, corresponding to our Senate, and consisting of forty-four deputies of the twenty-two cantons (which constituted the old Diet), and the *Nationalrath*, or House of Representatives, elected by the vote of the people according to population (one to every 20,000 souls). The executive department or *Bundesrath* consists of seven members, appointed by the two branches of the legislature for three years. They constitute the cabinet. The President (*Bundespräsident*) and the Vice-President of the republic are not elected by the people, as in the United States, but by the cabinet out of their number, and only for one year. The judicial department or supreme court (*Bundesgericht*) consists of eleven judges elected by the legislature for three years, and decides controversies between the cantons, etc.[1]

The constitution of 1848 was again revised and still more centralized May 29, 1874, with reference to the relation of the Federal government to railroads, post, and telegraphs, liberty of commerce, emigration, etc. The revision was sub-

von Tell" (*says Bluntschli, I., 69*), *" welcher den Vogt Gessler erschoss, weil er in ihm den freien Mann verhöhnt und den Vater geschändet hatte, enthält, wenn sie auch im Verfolg sagenhaft geschmückt wurde, doch einen ächten Zug des schweizerischen Nationalcharakters, und ist desshalb auch so populär geworden."*

[1] Comp. Rüttimann : " Das nordamerikanische Bundesstaatsrecht verglichen mit den politischen Einrichtungen der Schweiz." Zürich, 1867–72. 2 vols.

mitted to the vote of the people and accepted April 10, 1874, by 340,199 votes against 198,013, and by fourteen and a half of the cantons.

The Constitution of 1848 guaranteed "the free exercise of divine worship to the recognized confessions " (*i. e.* the Roman Catholic and Reformed), but forbade the order of the Jesuits.[1] The Constitution of 1874 goes further and comes nearer the American Constitution by declaring, without qualification, that freedom of belief and conscience are inviolable, that no one can be forced to accept or support a religion, or be punished on account of religious views, and that the free exercise of worship is secured within the limits of morality and public safety.[2] But the same Constitution, like that of 1848, excludes the order of the Jesuits and affiliated orders from Swiss territory, and prohibits their members to exercise any kind of activity in church or school.[3] The same prohibition may be extended to other spiritual orders which are deemed dangerous to the state or which disturb the peace of the confessions.[4] The Constitution for-

---

[1] Arts. 44 and 58.

[2] Art. 49. " *Die Glaubens- und Gewissensfreiheit ist unverletzlich—Niemand darf zur Theilnahme an einer Religionsgenossenschaft, oder an einem religiösen Unterricht, oder zur Vornahme einer religiösen Handlung gezwungen, order wegen Glaubensansichten mit Strafen irgend welcher Art belegt werden. Ueber die religiöse Erziehung der Kinder bis zum erfüllten 16. Altersjahr verfügt im Sinne vorstehender Grundsätze der Inhaber der väterlichen oder vormundschaftlichen Gewalt. Die Ausübung bürgerlicher oder politischer Rechte darf durch keinerlei Vorschriften oder Bedingungen kirchlicher oder religiöser Natur beschränkt werden. Die Glaubensansichten entbinden nicht von der Erfüllung der bürgerlichen Pflichten. Niemand ist gehalten, Steuern zu bezahlen, welche speciell für eigentliche Kultuszwecke einer Religionsgenossenschaft, der er nicht angehört, auferlegt werden.*"

Art. 50. " *Die freie Ausübung gottesdienstlicher Handlungen ist innerhalb der Schranken der Sittlichkeit und der öffentlichen Ordnung gewährleistet.*"

[3] Art. 51. " *Der Orden der Jesuiten und die ihm affiliirten Gesellschaften dürfen in keinem Theile der Schweiz Aufnahme finden, und es ist ihren Gliedern jede Wirksamkeit in Kirche und Schule untersagt.*"

[4] Art. 51, Sec. 2. " *Dieses Verbot kann durch Bundesbeschluss auch auf andere geistliche Orden ausgedehnt werden, deren Wirksamkeit staatsgefährlich ist oder den Frieden der Konfessionen stört.*" Under this restriction the Salvation Army was scandalously persecuted in several places of republican Switzerland in 1883 and 1884.

bids moreover the establishment of new or the re-establishment of abolished convents and religious orders.[1]

These restrictions are un-American, and an abridgment of religious liberty.

There is another important difference between the two countries. The principle of religious liberty has not yet worked its way into the several cantons of Switzerland. Each canton has still its own established church—either Roman Catholic or Reformed—supported and ruled by the civil magistrate. In recent times the politicians and so-called "reformers" have controlled the church in the interest of prevailing rationalism, and have forced the faithful adherents of the Reformation creeds to found free churches, in Geneva, the Canton de Vaud, and Neuchatel. The advanced liberal or radical party in Switzerland is very illiberal and intolerant towards positive Christianity. It would be far better if the connection between church and state in the different cantons were dissolved, and religion allowed to take its natural course. But the politicians will not surrender their control over religion.

The free churches in French Switzerland have shown a high decree of spiritual vitality and liberality.

The German Empire.

The German Empire, which arose under the leadership of Prussia from the brilliant victories over Austria in 1866, and over France in 1870, was proclaimed, by a striking nemesis of history, at Versailles in the palace of the persecutor of the Huguenots, the destroyer of the Palatinate and the robber of Alsace, Louis XIV., Jan. 18, 1871.[2] It marks an immense progress of liberty over the German Roman Empire, which lasted eight hundred years, from the coronation of Charle-

---

[1] Art. 52. "*Die Errichtung neuer und die Wiederherstellung aufgehobener Klöster oder religiöser Orden ist unzulässig.*" .

[2] The historian Leopold von Ranke is reported to have said, in reply to a question of Mons. Thiers during the Franco-German war in 1870, that Germany was making war, not upon Napoleon, not upon the French republic, least of all upon the French nation—but upon Louis XIV. Thiers, himself a distinguished historian, wondered at the long memory of the Germans.

magne by Pope Leo III. (800), to the resignation of Francis II. (1806), and over the feeble German Confederacy, which after a brief interregnum succeeded it for a short period (1815–1866).

The German Empire differs widely from the American Republic by its monarchical basis and hereditary principle, but nevertheless resembles it in several important respects. Both owe their origin to secular causes, and emerged success-fully from a war of self-defence, the one against Great Britain, the other against France. Both are compact federal states,[1] with a strong central sovereignty which acts directly upon the people, as distinct from a loose confederacy of indepen-dent States,[2] such as were the ancient leagues of Greece, the American Confederation before 1787, the Swiss Confederacy before 1848, and the German *Bund* which expired in 1866. Both are confined to political and civil interests, and have no direct or official connection with the church, but leave reli-gion to the several States, and dare not interfere with them. Every State of Germany has its own independent state church, with more or less toleration for " sects." There is no such thing as an imperial church (*Reichskirche*), any more than there is a national American church; there is not even such an organic connection between the different Protestant churches of the same confession, as exists in the United States.[3] Each church is confined to the geographical bound-aries of the State. *Cujus regio ejus religio.* This condition dates from the Diet of Spire, 1526, which allowed every Ger-man State to act on the question of the Reformation accord-ing to its own sense of duty to God and the emperor. The Westphalia Treaty of 1648 confirmed the equal rights of the two contending churches. But the Pope never consented to even this limited toleration and will always protest against it. The Papal Syllabus of 1864 condemns religious toleration among the eighty heresies of the age. The Roman Church

---

[1] *Bundesstaat.*   [2] *Staatenbund.*

[3] The only quasi-official bond of union between them is the so-called Eise-nach Conference, which meets once a year at Eisenach for the purpose of secur-ing co-operation in a few matters of general interest, such as the revision of the Luther Bible.

acknowledges no other church, and cannot do it consistently. She knows no geographical and national boundaries, and rallies around the common centre of the Vatican "vicegerent of God on earth." She must submit, of course, to hard necessity, but does it under protest: *Non possumus.*

The Constitution of the German Empire, dated April 14, 1871, if we except the words, "of God's grace" (*von Gottes Gnaden*), attached to the name of the emperor, says nothing about religion, and requires no religious tests as qualification for civil and political offices under the national government. Consequently the imperial Parliament is accessible to men of all creeds or of no creed.[1]

The principle of the freedom of conscience and worship, and the equality of the religious confessions before the law was first proclaimed as one of the fundamental rights of the German people by the Frankfort Parliament in 1849, and adopted by several States (Prussia, Saxony, etc.). The North German *Bund*, by an imperial law of July 3, 1869, proclaimed the same principle, and abolished all remaining restrictions of civil and political rights on account of religion which existed in the various States.[2] This law passed into the legislation of the whole empire in 1871.[3]

---

[1] "Verfassung des deutschen Reichs von Dr. Ludwig von Rönne." Berlin, 3d ed., 1878.

[2] The law of July 3, 1869, is as follows : "*Alle noch bestehenden, aus der Verschiedenheit des religiösen Bekenntnisses hergeleiteten Beschränkungen der bürgerlichen und staatsbürgerlichen Rechte werden hierdurch aufgehoben. Insbesondere soll die Befähigung zur Theilnahme an der Gemeinde- und Landesvertretung zur Bekleidung öffentlicher Aemter vom religiösen Bekenntniss unabhängig sein.*"

[3] Dr. L. von Rönne, "Das Staatsrecht des deutschen Reiches" (2d ed., Leipzig, 1877, 2 vols.), vol. i. p. 176: "*Die Verfassung des Deutschen Reiches enthält zwar keine Bestimmung über die Glaubens- und Religionsfreiheit im Reiche, allein schon das Reichsgesetz vom 1 November, 1867, über die Freizügigkeit, welches im ganzen Gebiete des Reiches Geltung hat, bestimmt im § 1, dass keinem Reichsangehörigen um des* GLAUBENSBEKENNTNISSES *willen der Aufenthalt, die Niederlassung, der Gewerbebetrieb oder der Erwerb von Grundeigenthum verweigert werden darf. Der hierdurch anerkannte Grundsatz der Glaubens und Religionsfreiheit hat demnächst seinen erweiterten Ausdruck gefunden in dem Reichsgesetze vom 3 Juli, 1869, betreffend die Gleichberechtigung der Konfessionen in bürgerlicher und staatsbürgerlicher Beziehung. Dieses*

So far the German Empire is committed to the principle of religious liberty and equality as much as the United States, and can as little interfere with the religious convictions and the exercise of public worship, or deny to any citizen his civil and political rights on account of his religious opinions. The only restriction in both countries is, that a man's religion cannot excuse him from the duties of citizenship.

für das Gebiet des Norddeutschen Bundes erlassene Gesetz trat in Folge des Art. 80, Ziffer 1, Nr. 20 der mit Baden und Hessen vereinbarten Bundesverfassung mit dem 1 Januar, 1871, auch in Baden und Südhessen, ferner von demselben Zeitpunkte an, zufolge des Art. 1 und des Art. 2, Nr. 6 des Bündnissvertrages vom 25 November, 1870, auch in Würtemberg, und endlich in Bayern zufolge des § 2, Ziffer 1, Nr. 10 des Reichsgesetzes vom 22 April, 1871, vom Tage der Wirksamkeit dieses Reichsgesetzes an in Kraft. Dagegen ist die Einführung des Gesetzes in dem Reichslande Elsass-Lothringen nicht erfolgt. Das Gesetz bestimmt, dass alle im Geltungsbereiche desselben noch bestehenden, aus der Verschiedenheit des religiösen Bekenntnisses hergeleiteten Beschränkungen der bürgerlichen und staatsbürgerlichen Rechte aufgehoben werden, und dass insbesondere die Befähigung zur Theilnahme an der Gemeinde- und Landesvertretung und zur Bekleidung öffentlicher Aemter vom religiösen Bekenntnisse unabhängig sein soll.''

Comp. Georg Meyer, "Lehrbuch des deutschen Staatsrechtes" (Leipzig, 1878), pp. 575 *sqq.*, and 610, "*Die Reichsgesetzgebung*" (he says, p. 610) "*hat, indem sie allen Reichsangehörigen das Recht der freien Niederlassung im ganzen Reichsgebiet gewährleistet, und jede aus der Verschiedenheit der Confessionen fliessende Ungleichheit der bürgerlichen und politischen Rechte ausschliesst, den Einzelstaaten die Befugniss entzogen, bestimmten Religionsgesellschaften die Aufnahme im Staatsgebiet zu verweigern. Die Reprobation einer Religionsgesellschaft kann künftighin nur im Wege der Reichsgesetzgebung stattfinden. Dagegen ist reichsgesetzlich weder eine allgemeine Freiheit der Bildung von Religionsvereinen, noch eine Gleichheit der Religionsübung für alle Confessionen garantirt. Vielmehr weisen in diesem Punkte die Landesgesetzgebungen grosse Verschiedenheiten auf. Einige geben die Bildung von Religionsgesellschaften unbedingt frei und gewähren allen volle häusliche und öffentliche Religionsübung. Nach diesen äussert sich das Reformationsrecht des Staates nur noch in der Ertheilung von Corporationsrechten und der Verleihung besonderer Privilegien. Andere gewähren zwar das Recht der freien Vereinigung zu religiösen Gemeinschaften, dagegen keine Gleichheit der Religionsübung; die Art derselben richtet sich nach den besonderen Verwilligungen. Noch andere endlich haben an dem Erforderniss staatlicher Genehmigung für die Bildung von religiösen Gemeinschaften festgehalten.*" For further consultation I may refer to Paul Laband, "Das Staatsrecht des deutschen Reiches" (Tübingen, 1876–82, 3 vols.), vol. i. pp. 161 *sq.*

In one instance, however, the Empire has, from patriotic motives, interfered with religion, namely, in the expulsion of the Jesuits from German territory, by an imperial law of July 4, 1872.[1] This was an act in self-defence against the political ambition and agitation of the hierarchical party under the lead of the Jesuits, who own no country except the church, and no loyalty except to the Pope. But it is nevertheless an infringement of religious liberty. Such an expulsion would be unconstitutional in the United States, unless the Jesuits by overt acts should endanger the public peace and safety.

In the several States which compose the Empire, the union of the state with the recognized confessions, *i. e.*, the Roman Catholic and the Evangelical (Lutheran and Reformed) Churches continues. Dissenting sects enjoy the rights of private corporations.[2]

Germany allows the greatest freedom of thought, but is very conservative in action. In no country is theological speculation and investigation so freely carried on and encouraged as in German universities under the patronage of the government, and in no country is a certain degree of education more general; for the laws of Prussia and nearly all other German States provide for the establishment of elementary schools in every town and village, and compel parents to send their children to these or private schools. And yet the most opposite parties in theology, from strict Lutheran orthodoxy to rationalism, prefer to remain under

[1] See Schulthess, "Europäischer Geschichtskalender" for 1872, p. 164.

[2] Meyer, *l. c.*, p. 611: "*Die katholische und die evangelische (lutherische und reformirte) Kirche nehmen die Stellung privilegirter Religionsgemeinschaften ein und gelten als öffentliche Corporationen. Sie geniessen einen besonderen strafrechtlichen Schutz, ihre Geistlichen sind in vielen Beziehungen den Staatsbeamten gleichgestellt, sie erhalten eine Dotation aus Staatsmitteln und ihre Abgaben können im Wege der Verwaltungsexecution beigetrieben werden. Den Katholiken stehen die Altkatholiken gleich, welche vom Standpunkte des Staates als Katholiken zu betrachten sind.*

"*Unter den übrigen christlichen Religionsgesellschaften sind diejenigen besonders ausgezeichnet, welche sich im Besitz von Corporationsrechten befinden. . . . Diejenigen Religionsgemeinschaften, welche Corporationsrechte nicht besitzen, haben den Charakter gewöhnlicher Vereine.*"

the same state-church roof of protection and support, and look with distrust or contempt upon the "sects."

Nevertheless some of these sects are spreading, in numbers and respectability, and the "Old Catholics," too, have become a distinct organization with government recognition in Prussia (1875) and Baden (1874).

The religious statistics of the German Empire, which numbers a population of over forty-six millions, according to the census of Dec. 1, 1880, are as follows:

Protestants	28,330,967	
Roman Catholics	16,232,606	
"Christian Sects"	78,395 [1]	
Jews	561,612	
"No religion"	30,481	

By "Protestants" are meant three denominations supported and governed by the state, Lutherans, German Reformed, and United Evangelical. The last is the largest, being the state-church of Prussia and of those minor States (Baden, Württemberg, etc.) which have adopted the union of the Lutheran and Reformed Churches. "The Christian sects" are Mennonites, Moravians, Irvingites, Methodists, Baptists, and others, who support and govern themselves, or are supported by their brethren in England and America. The "Old Lutherans" are seceders from the state-churches in Prussia and Saxony, and figure in the statistics among the sects, although they are the most orthodox among Protestants.

Prussia.

Prussia stands at the head of the German States and has the controlling influence in the German Empire. Her king is by hereditary right also Emperor of Germany. She has in theory been always very tolerant and allowed the utmost liberty of opinion within the state-church, but the exercise of public worship and the organization of dissenting communities was controlled and restricted by law till 1850.[2]

[1] This is too small an estimate.

[2] The *Allgemeine Landrecht* of Prussia, in agreement with the spirit of Frederick the Great, declares (Tit. xi. §§ 2 and 3): "*Jedem Einwohner im*

"The great Elector" offered a hospitable asylum to the expelled Huguenots of France, at a time when the Calvinists were denounced by orthodox Lutherans as dangerous heretics. Frederick II., the "alte Fritz," one of the demi-gods of the German people, was an admirer of Voltaire's philosophy of toleration (though he despised the man), and wished every Prussian to get saved "after his own fashion"; yet he commanded the celebrated Pietist, Dr. Francke in Halle, to go to the theatre which he had denounced, and ordered a clergyman, Frommann (Piousman), to change his name into Frohmann (Merryman).

There are three recognized churches in Prussia, the Lutheran, the German Reformed, and the Roman Catholic. The first two were consolidated into one by Frederick William III., in 1817, under the name of the United Evangelical Church. The House of Hohenzollern belongs originally to the German Reformed Church, but is now identified with the United Evangelical Church. The union was opposed by the "Old Lutherans," who seceded and were at first harshly dealt with by the government, but achieved liberty under Frederick William IV. (1845). The Evangelical Union, as officially explained (1834 and 1852), does not obliterate the doctrinal distinction of the two confessions, nor interfere with personal convictions, but requires both to live under one form of government, to use the same liturgy, and to commune together at the same altar. But the last feature, *die Abendmahlsgemeinschaft*, is offensive to the conscience of strict Lutherans, who reject the Reformed theory of the Lord's Supper as a heresy. The Lutherans of the newly acquired provinces of Schleswig-Holstein, Lauenburg, Hanover, Frankfort, etc., are not formally incorporated in the union, but subject to the same central government of the King and his Cultus-Minister.

Staate muss eine vollkommene Glaubens- und Gewissensfreiheit gestattet werden. Niemand ist schuldig über seine Privatmeinungen in Religionssachen Vorschriften vom Staate anzunehmen." But liberty is here restricted to *private* opinions which lie beyond the jurisdiction of the state, and may be enjoyed under the most despotic government. *" Gedanken sind zollfrei."*

Smaller religious communions enjoy the rights of private corporations by special concessions of the government.

According to the census of December 1, 1880, the total population of Prussia numbered 27,279,111 souls, classified as follows:

Protestants . . . . 17,613,530 (64 %)
Roman Catholics . . . . . . 9,205,136 (33 %)
Jews 363,790

The rest belong to smaller Christian " sects," or to "no creed."

The Evangelical state-church, which numbers about eighteen millions, or nearly two thirds of the population, is reduced to a department of state and connected, under one head (the Cultus-Minister), with the department of education and medical affairs. This is a humiliating position, to which the Roman Church would never submit. King Frederick William IV. (brother of Emperor William) felt painfully the weight of his position as *summus episcopus*, and frequently expressed his wish to restore the Evangelical Church to proper independence and self-government, with full toleration for dissenters; but his force was broken by the revolution of 1848.

The Prussian Constitution of January 31, 1850, marks a great progress in the line of religious liberty. It guarantees the freedom of conscience and *public worship*, and *independence*, in the administration of their internal affairs, to the Evangelical and Roman Catholic Churches, and *all other religious associations*, subject only to the civil and political duties. As to education, the Protestant children should be instructed in religion by the Protestant clergy; the Roman Catholic children by the Roman Catholic clergy, and the Jews by their rabbis.[1]

The most important provision is Article XII., which guarantees the three essential elements of religious and civil fredom : 1, the freedom of private and public worship ;

[1] See the Prussian *Verfassungs-Urkunde* of 1850, articles XII., XIII., XIV., XV., XVI., XVIII., XXIV. Similar provisions had been made by the famous national assembly of Frankfurt in 1849, in Art. V. of the *Grundrechte des deutschen Volkes.*

2, the right of religious association; 3, the enjoyment of civil and political rights, irrespective of religious views. The last implies separation of church and state as far as civil and political offices are concerned.[1]

Prussia has thus taken the lead in this progress of modern culture, and prescribed the course of the German Empire. One of the most eminent writers on law in Prussia, in commenting on the twelfth article, remarks that Prussia has constitutionally recognized perfect religious liberty as " the noblest fundamental right of every citizen," not in the spirit of religious indifference, but as the ripe fruit of a development of more than a hundred years, as a victory of justice and of a truly Christian view of life. He adds that it is the merit of the North Americans to have first proclaimed this principle as a constitutional law.[2]

But while this great principle remains, the independence of the recognized confessions in the management of their own affairs, which was likewise guaranteed, in Articles XV. and XVIII., was endangered, modified, and in part abolished during the so-called *Culturkampf*, or the conflict of modern culture with mediæval obscurantism, which has agitated Germany since 1870.

---

[1] Article XII. is as follows : " *Die Freiheit des religiösen Bekenntnisses, der Vereinigung zu Religionsgesellschaften und der gemeinsamen häuslichen und öffentlichen Religionsübung wird gewährleistet. Der Genuss der bürgerlichen und staatsbürgerlichen Rechte ist unabhängig von dem religiösen Bekenntnisse. Den bürgerlichen und staatsbürgerlichen Pflichten darf durch die Ausübung der Religionsfreiheit kein Abbruch geschehen.*" Comp. L. v. Rönne, "Das Staatsrecht der Preussischen Monarchie" (Leipzig, 3d ed., 1869–72), vol. i., Abth. ii. p. 167 *sqq.;* and H. Schulze, "Das Preussische Staatsrecht" (Leipzig, 1872, 77, 2 vols.), vol. i. pp. 398 *sqq.*

[2] Hermann Schulze (Prof. of Jurisprudence in the University of Breslau, and member of the Prussian House of Lords), "Das Preussische Staatsrecht," vol. i. pp. 405 *sq.:* " *So ist vollkommene religiöse Bekenntnissfreiheit, als das edelste Grundrecht aller Staatsgenossen, in Preussen verfassungsmässig anerkannt, nicht als Zeichen religiöser Gleichgültigkeit, sondern als gereifte Frucht einer mehr als hundertjährigen Staatsentwicklung, als Sieg deutscher Gerechtigkeit und wahrhaft christlicher Lebensanschauung. . . . Den Nordamericanern gebührt das Verdienst, zuerst die Religionsfreiheit als Verfassungsgesetz verkündigt zu haben, nachdem Friedrich der Grosse dieselbe theoretisch vertheidigt und praktisch gehandhabt hatte.*"

This important and interesting conflict was provoked by the aggressions of Romanism, as shown in the Papal Syllabus of 1864, which declared open war to all the liberal ideas of the age, in the passage of the infallibility dogma of the Vatican Council in 1870, and in the open hostility of the Ultramontane party to the new German Empire with a Protestant head. In some respects the *Culturkampf* is a renewal of the old war between the emperor and the pope, or state-craft and priestcraft. It developed the singular anomaly that the Protestant Liberals (the so-called National Liberal party in the German Diet and the Prussian Chambers) attacked the liberty and independence of the church ; while the Roman Catholics (guided by the Centre party in the Diet) defended the freedom of the church, to be sure only in their own interest, and in the hierarchical sense of the term. The leaders of political liberalism in Germany and all over the Continent are religiously illiberal, or unchurchly and anti-churchly, and wish to keep the church, both Catholic and Protestant, under the thumb of the state. They confound clericalism and priestcraft with all forms of positive Christianity. On the other hand the majority of orthodox Protestants are conservative in politics. In the *Culturkampf* they were either passive spectators, or aided in the enactment of the May-Laws, from opposition to Rome, without considering that thereby they weakened their own right and claim to independence. The misfortune of Germany is the unnatural alliance of religion with political conservatism, and of liberalism with infidelity. This is largely the effect of state-church coercion. In Great Britain and the United States Christianity is friendly to political and all other progress, and takes the lead in every moral reform.

The *Culturkampf* centred in Prussia, and the prophecy of Cardinal Wiseman, that the war between Romanism and Protestantism will be fought out on the sand of Brandenburg, seemed to approach its fulfilment. Prussia felt the necessity of protecting herself against the political ambition of the hierarchy. In order to do this constitutionally, the Prussian legislature (*Landtag*), April 5, 1873, changed those articles which guaranteed the independence of the church, as follows, the changes being indicated by italics :

Article XV.—" The Evangelical and the Roman Catholic Church, as well as every other religious association, shall administer independently its own affairs, *but remains subject to the laws and to the legally regulated supervision of the state.*

" *In the same measure* each religious association shall remain in possession and enjoyment of the establishments, endowments, and funds devoted to the purposes of worship, education, and benevolence."

Article XVIII.—" The right of the state to nominate, propose, elect, and ratify appointments to ecclesiastical positions is hereby abolished, unless the right rests upon patronage or some other legal title.

" This provision shall not apply to the appointment of chaplains in the army or clergymen in public [*i. e.*, governmental] establishments.

" *As to the rest, the law regulates the functions of the state in reference to the education, appointment, and dismissal of the clergy and the servants of the church, and determines the limits of the disciplinary power of the church."* [1]

These changes neutralized the force of the original articles or reduced them to a mere shadow. But even this shadow disappeared. Two years later, April 10, 1875, the *Landtag* abolished articles XV., XVI., and XVIII. altogether, and thus freed the government from every constitutional limitation in dealing with the church question.[2] This is, from

[1] Artikel XV.—" Die evangelische und die römisch-katholische Kirche, sowie jede andere Religionsgesellschaft ordnet und verwaltet ihre Angelegenheiten selbstständig, *bleibt aber den Staats-Gesetzen und der gesetzlich geordneten Aufsicht des Staates unterworfen.*

" *Mit der gleichen Massgabe* bleibt jede Religionsgesellschaft im Besitz und Genuss der für ihre Kultus-, Unterrichts-, und Wohlthätigkeits-Zwecke bestimmten Anstalten, Stiftungen und Fonds."

Artikel XVIII.—" Das Ernennungs-, Vorschlags-, Wahl- und Bestätigungs-Recht bei Besetzung kirchlicher Stellen ist, soweit es dem Staat zusteht und nicht auf dem Patronat oder besondern Rechtstiteln beruht aufgehoben.

" Auf Anstellung von Geistlichen beim Militair und an öffentlichen Anstalten findet diese Bestimmung keine Anwendung.

" *Im Uebrigen regelt das Gesetz die Befugnisse des Staats hinsichtlich der Vorbildung, Anstellung und Entlassung der Geistlichen und Religionsdiener und stellt die Grenzen der kirchlichen Disciplinargewalt fest."*

See Schulthess, " Eur. Gesch.kalender " for 1873, pp. 36–45. Dr. Paul Hinschius (Professor of Jurisprudence in Berlin, who helped to frame the May-Laws), " Die Preussischen Kirchengesetze des Jahres, 1873," p. xxix. They give also the May-Laws.

[2] The repeal was proclaimed by edict, dated Bad Ems, June 18, 1875 : " We William, of God's grace King of Prussia, etc., order, with the consent of both

the American standpoint, a retrograde step and a relapse into Erastianism and state-despotism.

The Anti-Papal Laws.

The ominous change of the constitution in 1873 was followed in May of the same year, under the direction of Dr. Falk, the liberal minister of public worship and instruction, by the enactment of the so-called four May-Laws, or Falk-Laws, whose object was to restrict the disciplinary power of the Roman Church and to raise up a cultured and patriotic clergy. Pope Pius IX., in letters to Emperor William, to the German bishops, and by an Encyclical of February 5, 1875, denounced these laws in the strongest terms as " contrary to the divine constitution of the church," and declared them " null and void." The Prussian bishops openly disobeyed them. This conduct forced the government into supplementary legislation in 1874 and 1875, enabling the state to carry out the May-Laws. The details are not necessary for our purpose.[1]

The anti-papal laws were intended only for Prussia, as temporary measures of self-protection, but indirectly they affected also the whole Empire. Prince Bismarck conducted the negotiations with Pope Leo as prime minister of Prussia, not as chancellor of the empire; but he is, in fact, the head of both under William I., who is king and emperor; and to expel the disobedient bishops from Germany he had to get authority from the imperial diet.

In this conflict the Prussian government, blinded by its traditional state-absolutism, undervalued the strength of the Roman Church and exceeded its legitimate power by interfering with her internal affairs, in attempting to control even the theological education of the priesthood. Although the Roman Church in Prussia numbers only about ten mil-

houses of the *Landtag* of our monarchy, as follows : Articles XV., XVI., and XVIII. of the *Verfassungsurkunde* of Jan. 31, 1850, are abolished." The XVIth article guarantees freedom of intercourse between the religious associations and their ecclesiastical superior (the Pope).

[1] They are fully explained by Professor Hinschius in the second volume of his work on the " Prussian Church Laws " (1875).

lions in a population of twenty-eight millions, she is a consolidated phalanx, backed by the most powerful organization
centering in the papacy.   Behind this organization are
those invisible religious forces which lie beyond the jurisdiction of the government and the efficiency of state laws.
The government saw in the hierarchy only a political oppo-
nent, and tried to conquer it by political power.   Moreover,
the state made the innocent suffer with the guilty, and did
an act of gross injustice to the Evangelical Church, which
was included in this Erastian legislation, although she had
done nothing whatever to deserve such an indirect rebuke.

For seven years (1873–1880) the May-Laws were rigidly
executed, and disobedient bishops deposed and exiled.
The imperial government came to the aid of Prussia, and
authorized by a law of May 4, 1874, their banishment from
German territory.   The Pope answered by crowning two of
the " martyrs " with the cardinal's hat.   In 1877 eight of the
twelve Prussian bishoprics were vacant, and about four hundred parishes were without priests.   This state of things
threatened general confusion and could not last long.   Persecution gave the Roman Church the glory of martyrdom
and the credit of fighting for the freedom of the church.
She was supported by the laity, who were left like flocks
without shepherds.

The government began to feel that the May-Laws could
not be maintained and executed without the greatest danger
to the state.   In the meantime the National Liberal party
began to break up in factions; the socialists made two attempts on the life of the aged emperor, and revealed a
more dangerous power to the state than even ultramontan-
ism.   Prince Bismarck left the National Liberal party, with
whose help he had completed the organization of the
empire, and built up a conservative party.   Emperor William
was anxious to make peace with the church before his death,
and the Empress, who is on good terms with the bishops,
moved behind the curtain in the same direction.   In the
Roman Church, too, a great change took place by the death
of Pius IX. (1878), with whom nothing could be done, and

the accession of Leo XIII., who understands the policy of accommodation to existing circumstances, and showed from the start a disposition to come to a peaceful understanding with the central power of Europe.

Under these circumstances, the Prussian government, in 1880, asked and obtained permission from the *Landtag* to suspend the execution of the May-Laws in order to meet the spiritual wants of the Catholic laity, who were innocent and yet suffered most. The laws were suspended during 1880 and 1881. In February, 1882, the government went a step further and entered into negotiations with the Pope through a special ambassador, Herr von Schlözer, who had formerly been in Washington. These negotiations resulted in the gradual repeal of the May-Laws, which was completed April 29, 1887, so that nothing remains of them except the law of 1872 which makes civil marriage obligatory and sufficient, the laws of 1875 and 1876 regulating the adminis-tration of church property, the law prohibiting the exercise of church discipline by foreign tribunals, and the *An-zeigepflicht*, or the duty of notification, which requires the Pope and the bishops to inform the government of ecclesi-astical appointments and concedes to the state the right of veto on grounds of civil or political disabilities of the appointees.

No principle was surrendered, but a *modus vivendi* was secured for a peaceful coëxistence of a sovereign state and a sovereign church.[1]

[1] On the recent conflict between Prussia and the papacy, see Prof. Paul Hinschius, " Die Preussischen Kirchengesetze des Jahres 1873 " (Berlin, 1873); by the same, " Die Preussischen Kirchengesetze der Jahre 1874 und 1875, nebst dem Reichsgesetze vom 4 Mai, 1874 " (Berlin, 1875). A learned com-mentary and defence of the anti-papal laws. Comp. also, his supplements (1886 and 1887). Dr. Kries, " Die Preussische Kirchengesetzgebung," etc., (Danzig, 1887). " Les discours de M. le Prince de Bismarck," vol. iv., under the separate title : " Kulturkampf. Histoire du conflict politique-clérical en Prusse et en Allemagne depuis son origine jus qu' à ce jour (1871–1887)," etc., Berlin, 1887. Contains all the documents. R. Majunke (R. Cath.), " Ge-schichte des Culturkampfes in Preussen-Deutchland," Paderborn, 1887. On the general subject, see F. Heinrich Geffcken, " Staat und Kirche in ihrem Verhältniss geschichtlich entwickelt," Berlin, 1875. Wilhelm Martens, " Die

Prince Bismarck, the Luther of regenerated Germany, who once protested that he would "never go to Canossa," made peace with Pope Leo, meeting him half-way, but securing in return his political services in the septennate conflict of 1887 against the threatening war of revenge from France and the socialistic revolution from within. The Pope sent to the Protestant heretic the Christ-order, a distinction shown only to most eminent Catholic celebrities. Leo out-bismarcked Bismarck, and Bismarck out-poped the Pope.

For the present the *Culturkampf* has ended with a substantial victory of the Roman Church under the wise and moderate statesmanship of Leo XIII. She is now stronger than ever in Germany; for how long, God only knows. Abuse of power will inevitably provoke reactions.

The Evangelical Church, unfortunately, remains in Prussia, as in all Germany, an humble servant of the state, and is much weakened by internal dissensions. The success of the Roman Church has raised a new party among the conservative and churchly members of the *Landtag*, who demand from the government more liberty and more money, but without much prospect of getting either. The Protestant church cannot expect to secure the right of self-government without discharging the duty of self-support.

During the course of this memorable conflict between the Prussian government and the Roman curia the separation of church and state seems not to have occurred to the cultured leaders of either party as a possible solution of the problem. To be sure, it would be contrary to Prussian traditions, and involve two great sacrifices: the state would have to surrender its entire control over the churches, and the churches would have to surrender all claim upon the support of the state, whether the state were willing to restore the church property to its rightful owner or not. Perhaps,

Beziehungen der Ueberordnung, Nebenordnung und Unterordnung zwischen Kirche und Staat," Stuttgart, 1877. Meyer, "Lehrbuch des deutschen Staatsrechtes," Leipzig, 1878, p. 606 *sqq.* The ablest discussion of the *Culturkampf* in the English language, to my knowledge, is by Prof. John W. Burgess, "The Culturconflict in Prussia," in the *Political Science Quarterly* for June, 1887, p. 313 *sqq.* (New York).

after all, it may come to such a separation in due time. It would save the state and the church the troubles which inevitably arise from the collision of the two powers.

Scandinavia.

Denmark, Sweden, and Norway accepted the Lutheran creed with an episcopal organization. The great mass of the people are still strongly attached to the Lutheran Church, and honor it by their intelligence, industry, virtue, and piety, but are growing more liberal. Formerly every other religion was prohibited, on pain of confiscation and exile. Christina, the daughter of the illustrious Gustavus Adolphus, the Protestant hero of the Thirty Years' War, lost her crown and home by embracing the Roman Catholic faith.

At present the Lutheran Church is still the state church, and the kings of Denmark and Sweden must belong to it, but other churches are tolerated as "sects," and the civil disabilities have been gradually removed, in Denmark, by the constitution of June 5, 1849, modified in 1855, 1863, and July 28, 1866 ; in Sweden and Norway, by special laws in 1860, 1868, and 1873. The dissenters (Roman Catholics, Reformed, Baptists, Methodists, Irvingites, Jews, and Mormons) embrace only about one per cent. of the population in Denmark. But in Sweden the Baptists have grown very rapidly *within* the national church, and prefer to remain (like the Pietistic sects in Württemberg) an *ecclesiola in ecclesia*, because they have thus more liberty than outside of it. As a separate body they would, under the present dissenter law, have to purchase independence by asking recognition from the government, and subjecting themselves to its police regulations; while now they are allowed to build chapels, hold separate meetings, and baptize their converts by immersion, without disturbance, on condition of paying taxes for the support of the state church. This anomalous condition will probably end in secession as soon as the dissenter law is more liberalized. The Baptists in Sweden number in this year 1887 over 31,000 members, and have a theological school at Stockholm.

The Methodists in Sweden are a foreign plant, and derive their chief support from America, but commend themselves by their zeal for vital, practical piety.[1]

Austria.

Austria, under the rule of the Habsburg dynasty, has always been the political stronghold of Romanism in Germany, and granted only a very limited toleration to Protestants of the Augsburg and the Helvetic Confessions, and to the Socinians (Unitarians) in Transylvania.

Since 1848 she has entered upon a career of revolution and progress. A law of 1868 grants civil marriage and full liberty of religion, but within the limits of the confessions that are recognized by the government. The Roman Church remains the state religion and controls politics. It depends upon the prevailing sentiment of the provincial and local authorities how far the letter of the constitution can be executed or evaded. In 1879 the General Evangelical Alliance Conference of Basel sent a deputation to the Emperor Franz Josef I. in behalf of persecuted Protestants in Bohemia, and succeeded.

Since 1867 Austria is a bipartite state of Austria-Hungary, with a double legislature and double cabinet. In Austria proper, Romanism is still all-powerful. The government supports also Lutheran and Calvinistic ministers, but very scantily, and does not even admit the Protestant theological faculty of Vienna to a place in the corporation of the University and the use of its magnificent building.

In Hungary there is no state religion, and consequently more liberty. The Reformed (Calvinistic) Church is strong among the Magyars, and the Lutheran among the Germans; but the Roman Catholic is richer and stronger than both. Besides there are Greeks, Armenians, Jews, and "Non-Christians."

Holland.

Holland stands very high in the history of religious liberty. She achieved by her bravery and endurance her indepen-

---

[1] "Of all sectarian churches," says an orthodox Swedish Lutheran writer (in Herzog, vol. xiii., 743), "Methodism, by its open visor and moral earnestness, has acquired the greatest esteem in Sweden."

dence from the terrible despotism of Spain, which killed
more Protestants than heathen Rome killed Christians under
Nero or Decius or Domitian.   She sheltered the exiled band
of the " Pilgrim Fathers " before their departure for the bleak
coasts of New England.   It is true, the Calvinism of the
Synod of Dort (1619), in compact with Prince Maurice, is
responsible for the deposition and exile of about two hundred Arminian clergymen and of the great statesman and
scholar, Hugo Grotius.   But after the death of Maurice
(1625) the Arminians were recalled and allowed to build
churches in every town.

   The present kingdom of the Netherlands, according to the
terms of the constitution of November 3, 1848, grants entire
liberty of conscience and complete civil equality to the
members of all religious confessions.   The royal family and
a majority of the inhabitants belong to the Reformed
Church, which is the national church and supported by the
government ; but the Roman Catholic Church, and several
English Presbyterian ministers in the sea-ports, receive likewise government aid.   The national Reformed Church has
given up the canons of Dort and allows as wide a latitude of
thought to her theological professors and ministers as Protestant Germany and Switzerland.   Hence a number of strict
Calvinists have seceded and organized a free church (1834)
under the name of the " Christian Reformed Church," which
numbers several hundred congregations.   In 1857 the government, under the combined influence of the Romanists
and Liberals, banished all religious instruction from the
schools, and in 1876 it abolished the theological faculties in
the universities, retaining only such chairs as teach the history and philosophy of religion, and leaving the provision
for special theological instruction to the National Synod out
of funds granted to it.   When the Synod filled the professor-
ships with Rationalists, the orthodox Calvinistic party within the National Church established a Free Reformed University at Amsterdam (1880).   The same party has founded all
over Holland a large number of free schools in which religion
is taught.

France.[1]

The Latin races of Southern Europe rejected the Reformation, and reaped the Revolution. They preferred the yoke of popery to the liberty of the gospel, and ran into the opposite extreme of infidelity. They aspire to political liberty, but ignore religious liberty which is the strong pillar of the former. The French took the lead in crushing Protestantism by despotism, and crushing despotism by revolutions. They swing from the pope to Voltaire and back again to the pope, but never stop half way. They are the most polished, the most brilliant, and the most changeable nation of Europe.

The Edict of Nantes, which secured a legal existence to Protestants, was revoked by Louis XIV., and the Huguenots were forced to renounce their faith, or to leave their native land. But Protestantism survived the dragonades as "a church of the desert," regained toleration in 1787, and has remained ever since an intelligent, moral, industrious, and influential, though small, minority in France.

Since the radical upheaval of society in 1789, France has lived under nine constitutions (1791. 1793, 1795, 1799, 1814, 1830, 1848, 1852, 1875).

The principle of limited toleration has been acknowledged by all governments since Napoleon, but in subordination to the sovereignty of the State. Religious liberty as understood in England and America does not exist in France to this day. The advocates of political liberty (except among Protestants) are mostly indifferent or hostile to religion. Anti-clericalism with them means anti-religionism. The government supports and thereby controls a certain number of recognized religions.

[1] F. A. Hélie, " Les constitutions de la France," Paris, 1875. A. Bard et P. Robiquet, " La constitution française de 1875," Paris, 1878. E. Bidault, " Assemblées législatives de la France, 1789–1876," Paris, 1879. G. Demombynes, " Constitutions Européennes," Paris, 1881, 2 vols. E. de Pressensé, " L' église et la révolution française," Paris, 1867, and " La liberté religieuse en Europe depuis 1870," Paris, 1874. Francis Lieber gives several French constitutions, " On Civil Liberty and Self-Government " (Philad., 1859), p. 536 *sqq.*

This system dates from Napoleon I., the greatest military genius and despot on a democratic basis. He restored, in a measure, the Roman church in France after its overthrow by the madness of the Revolution. He was too much of a statesman not to see the absolute necessity of religion for society. But he felt no personal interest in it, and viewed it merely from the military and political point of view. " *Je ne vois pas,*" he said, " *dans la religion le mystère de l'incarnation, mais le mystère de l'ordre social.*" In Egypt he supported Mohammedanism, and placed the Koran along-side of the New Testament under the heading, " Politics." The priests he viewed as a sort of black policemen and as "*professeurs d' obéissance passive.*" Accordingly he recognized the Roman Catholic religion as the religion of the great majority of Frenchmen, and also the National Reformed and Lutheran Churches.[1] He made scanty provision for their support from the national treasury, by which he kept them subject to his power. To separate church and state after the American fashion would have limited his sovereignty. He would not listen to it for a moment. He concluded a concordat with Pope Pius VII. (July 15, 1801), and secured his consent to crown him emperor (Dec. 2, 1804); but he deprived him of his temporal power (May 17, 1809), and made him his prisoner at Fontainebleau (1812). His ambition was to rule the whole world from Paris, with the Pope residing there as his humble servant. But the haughty structure collapsed like the tower of Babel.

After the fall of Napoleon came the legitimist and papal reaction of the Bourbons, who, like the Stuarts, never forgot and never learned any thing, and who, like the Stuarts, by their reactionary and selfish policy prepared their own second and final overthrow.

The reign of the house of Orleans, which succeeded that of the Bourbons, was a limited constitutional monarchy and a compromise between the Revolution and the Restora-

---

[1] Against the protest of Pope Pius VII., whose secretary, Consalvi, made during the negotiations with Napoleon the characteristic admission : " *Il est de l'esssence de la religion catholique d'être intolerante.*" Haussonville, " Leglise romaine et le premier empire," vol. i. 308.

tion. It acknowledged to a limited extent the principle of religious liberty.

The charter of August 14, 1830, signed by King Louis Philippe and his prime minister, Guizot (a Protestant), provides that "each one may profess his religion with equal liberty, and shall receive for his religious worship the same protection" (Article V.), and that "the ministers of the catholic, apostolic, and Roman religion, professed by the majority of the French, and those of other Christian worship, receive stipends from the public treasury" (Article VI.).

The constitution of the second Republic of 1848, which followed the dethronement of Louis Philippe, guarantees that "every one may freely profess his own religion, and shall receive from the state equal protection in the exercise of his worship. The ministers of the religions at present recognized by law, as well as those which may be hereafter recognized, have a right to receive an allowance from the state" (Chap. II., Art. VII.).

The restoration of the Empire by Napoleon III. returned to the policy of the first Napoleon, but gave greater power to the Pope, and forced a new organization upon the recognized Protestant churches (1852). Like his uncle, he cut his own throat by his overreaching ambition, and went down with his empire at the battle of Sedan (Sept. 2, 1870). His only son and heir perished among the savages in Africa. His widow still lives, a modern Niobe, "crownless and childless in her voiceless woe."

A third Republic rose from the ruins of the second Empire (1870), and has lasted much longer than the first and second. The constitution adopted February 25, 1875, and still in force, says nothing on the subject of religious liberty, but the former system of cæsaro-papal rule and state patronage is continued. The Roman Church, the Reformed (Calvinistic), and the Lutheran Churches, and, since 1841, also the Jewish synagogue, and, in Algiers, the Mohammedan religion, are recognized by law and supported from the national treasury, but at the expense of their independence. Under the successful administration of Thiers, chiefly through the influence of Guizot, the Reformed Church was permitted to hold an official synod in 1872, but the government refused to sanction its decisions. The synods held since that time are " unofficial," and have no legislative power.

In the meantime free churches have sprung up, which support and govern themselves, and are tolerated. The chief among them (since 1849) is the " *Union des églises évangéliques de France,*" usually called " *l' église libre.*" The M'All " missions " (since 1871) are not organized churches and confine themselves to preaching the gospel; they are required by the police to abstain from politics and from attacks upon the Catholic Church. Other denominations, the Episcopalian, Presbyterian, Wesleyan, Baptist, etc., are of foreign origin and confined to a few congregations in Paris.

The French Republic has manifested a strong anti-clerical spirit and shown no favor to any religion. In this respect it contrasts very unfavorably with the American Republic. The possibilities for the future of France seem to be a conservative republic, or a socialistic revolution, or a restoration of the Orleans dynasty. The sympathies of America are with a conservative republic.

We may add from the " Statesman's Year-Book " for 1887 (pp. 66, 67), the following additional information :

" The population of France, at the census of December, 1881, consisted of 29,201,703 Roman Catholics, being 78.50 per cent. of the total population ; of 692,800 Protestants, or 1.8 per cent. of the population, as compared with 584,-757 in 1872 ; of 53,446 Jews, and 7,684,906 persons ' who declined to make any declaration of religious belief.' This was the first census at which ' non-professants ' were registered as such. On former occasions it had been customary to class all who had refused to state what their religion was, or who denied having any religion, as Roman Catholics. The number of persons set down as belonging to ' various creeds ' was 33,042.

" All religions are equal by law, and any sect which numbers 100,000 adherents is entitled to a grant ; but at present only the Roman Catholics, Protestants, Jews, and Mussulmans (Algeria, etc.) have state allowances. In the Budget for 1887 these grants were as follows :

	Francs.
Administration	257,800
Roman Catholic worship, etc, ...	44,327,123
Protestant worship, etc.	1,551,600
Jewish worship, etc.	180,900
Protestant and Jewish places of worship . . .	40,000
Mussulman worship	216,340
Total	46,573,763

" There are 17 archbishops and 67 bishops ; and of the Roman Catholic
Church on January, 1884, the secular clergy numbered in all 54,513, besides
10,464 pupils in the ecclesiastical seminaries.   The value of the total gifts and
legacies made to the Church during the present century, up to 1882, is 23,976,-
733 francs.   The Protestants of the Augsburg Confession, or Lutherans, are,
in their religious affairs, governed by a General Consistory, while the members
of the Reformed Church, or Calvinists, are under a council of administration,
the seat of which is at Paris.   In 1884 there were 700 Protestant pastors,
with 27 assistant preachers, and 57 Jewish rabbis and assistants."

Belgium.

Belgium, which was previously a part of Holland, has
formed since 1830 an independent state, and is a constitutional, representative, and hereditary monarchy.   Nearly the
whole population is nominally Roman Catholic, and divided
into six dioceses (Malines, Bruges, Ghent, Liège, Namur,
Tournai).   There is a constant conflict going on between the
ultramontane and the liberal Catholics.   The Protestants
number only 15,000, and the Jews 3,000.

The constitution of 1831 guarantees full religious liberty.
The government, like that of France, pays a part of the sal-
ary to Roman priests, Protestant ministers, and Jewish rabbis.   But there is also a free Reformed Church in Belgium
similar to that in France.   It is partly supported by friends
from abroad, and does faithful missionary work among the
lower Roman Catholic population.

Italy.

The year 1848 forms a turning-point in the history of
Italy.   The fundamental statute of Sardinia (*statuto fonda-
mentale del regno*), proclaimed by King Charles Albert at
Turin, March 4, 1848, declares the Roman Catholic Church
to be the only state religion, but grants toleration to other
existing forms of worship within the laws.[1]   The unification
of Italy, with Rome as the capital, in 1870, extended the
force of this statute over the whole kingdom.   Since that
time the legislature by several acts has diminished the power

[1] " *La religione Catholica Apostolica Romana è la sola religione dello stato.
Gli altri culti ora existenti sono tollerati conformemente alle leggi.*"   See Ga-
briello Carnazza :   " Il Diritto Costituzionale Italiano," Catania, 1886, p. 331.

of the church and clergy, and subordinated them to the authority of the civil government.

Cavour, the statesman; Mazzini, the dreamer; Garibaldi, the hero; and Victor Emanuel, the king, of regenerated Italy, were in favor of full religious liberty, though more from indifference than from an enlightened positive faith. A large number of educated men in Italy, as in all the Latin races, are indifferent and skeptical; but, knowing only the Roman religion, and wishing to be on the safe side in the other world, usually send for the priest on their death-bed. Even Voltaire did so.

Although toleration is a poor concession, it marks a great advance beyond the former state of disgraceful intolerance, when as late as 1852 the innocent Madiai family were imprisoned in Florence for no other crime than holding prayer-meetings and reading the Scriptures in the vernacular; when the Bible could not pass the custom-house in the Pope's dominions; and when the foreign Protestant residents of Rome were not allowed to worship God except in strict privacy, or in a house behind a barn outside of the city walls.

The statute of 1848 emancipated the faithful and much persecuted Waldenses; enabled them to preach in Italian, and to come out of their mountain fastnesses in Piedmont. Since 1870 there have been organized at least a dozen Protestant congregations in the city of Rome itself, which represent the Waldensian, the Free Italian Church (*chiesa libera*), the English and American Episcopal, the Scotch Presbyterian, the Methodist, the Baptist, the German Evangelical, and the French Reformed denominations. Such a variety is very confusing to the mind of an Italian Catholic is who discontented with Romanism, and yet used to the idea of the visible unity of the church.

The total number of Protestants in Italy at the census of 1881 amounted (in a population of nearly thirty millions) to 62,000, of whom 22,000 belonged to the Waldensian Church, and 30,000 to foreign Protestant bodies.

The kingdom of Italy sustains a peculiar relation to the papacy. It has destroyed its temporal power and thereby broken the backbone of hierarchical state-churchism. It has conquered the papal territory, made the papal capital its own capital, and thereby incurred the curses of the Pope who will forever protest against the robbery of the patrimony of St. Peter, in spite of the almost unanimous opposition of his own former subjects to the continuance of his secular rule.[1]

But by a decree of October 9, 1870, and the laws of December 31, 1870, and May 13, 1871, Italy guarantees to the supreme pontiff the dignity, inviolability, and all the personal prerogatives of a sovereign with the first rank among Catholic monarchs ; untrammelled correspondence with the Catholic hierarchy throughout the world ; the perpetual possession of the Vatican and Lateran palaces and castel-Gandolfo, with all the edifices, museums, libraries, and gardens belonging thereto ; freedom from taxation ; and an irrevocable annual dotation of 3,225,000 lire or francs from the public treasury.[2]

The Pope has refused the dotation, and can afford to live on the Peter's penny and other voluntary contributions of the faithful.

The political regeneration and unification of Italy has not materially changed the ruling religion of Italy, but has established a separation between the civil and spiritual powers and confined the papacy to the latter. Politically, the modern Italians are Protestants, and disregard the Pope in temporal matters ; religiously, they are Catholics, and obey him as the head of the church.

Spain and Portugal.

Spain, the land of sombre cathedrals and bloody bull-rings, the home of the Inquisition and Ignatius Loyola, is more intensely Roman Catholic and mediæval than Italy, and owing to its comparative isolation, is less influenced by modern ideas of progress. Cardinal Cuesta, Archbishop of Santiago,

---

[1] In the plebiscite, Oct. 2, 1870, the population of the Papal States voted with an overwhelming majority for annexation to the kingdom of Italy. The number of registered voters was 167,548 ; the number of actual voters, 135,291; of these 133,681 voted yea, 1,507 no ; 103 votes were thrown out as invalid. Schulthess, " Europäischer Geschichtskalender " for 1870 (Nördlingen, 1871), p. 403.   [2] Schulthess, *l. c.*, p. 410 *sqq.*

in a popular catechism, 1871, defines Protestantism to be "not only a veritable Babel, but a horrible theory, and an immoral practice which blasphemes God, degrades man, and endangers society."[1] The Reformation which raised its head in the middle of the sixteenth century, was completely crushed out by fire and sword under Philip II., and has only recently ventured to reappear. When Matamoras, Carrasco, and a few other converted Bible readers assembled for religious devotions, they were thrown into prison and condemned to the galleys, but in consequence of a strong protest by an international deputation of the Evangelical Alliance, the sentence of penal servitude was changed into exile (1863). A few years afterwards the misgovernment and immorality of the bigoted Queen Isabel II. resulted in her expulsion from the throne (1868), and a succession of revolutions and civil wars.

The Constitution of 1869 declares, in Article XXI., the Catholic Apostolic Roman Religion to be the religion of the state, and imposes upon the nation the obligation of maintaining its worship and its ministers. This is old Spanish. The second clause grants, for the first time, toleration for *public* and private worship to *foreigners* residing in Spain, subject to the general rules of morals and right. A third clause applies the same toleration to such Spaniards (if there should be any) as may profess another religion than the Catholic.[2]

---

[1] Bishop Manuel of the island of Minorca issued a manifesto, February 15, 1876, in which he demanded the expulsion of the children of Protestant parents from the public schools, or the compulsory memorizing of Cardinal Cuesta's Catechism against "the poison of Protestantism." Schulthess, "Europ. Geschichtskalender" for 1876, pp. 271 *sq.*

[2] "ART. XXI. *La religion católica, apostólica, romana es la del Estado. La Nacion se obliga á mantener el culto y los ministros de la religion católica.*

"*El ejercicio público ó privado de cualquiera otro culto queda garantido á todos los extranjeros residentes en España, sin más limitaciones que las reglas universales de la moral y del derecho.*

"*Si algunos españoles profesaren otra religion que la católica, es aplicable á los mismos todo lo dispuesto en el párafo anterior.*" See "Constituciones Vigentes de los principales estados de Europa." Por R. C. Ortiz y H. A. de Aparicio. Madrid, 1873, 2 vols., vol. ii., 308. Comp. Schulthess "Europäischer Geschichtskalender," 1870, pp. 299 *sq.* The articles XX. and XXI. were adopted by the Cortes May 5, 1869, by a majority of 164 to 4. The entire Constitution was adopted June 1st by a majority of 214 to 56 votes.

This was a small breach into the fort of Roman intolerance and exclusiveness. Another step in advance was taken by the Constitution adopted under the reign of Alphonso XII., July 1, 1876, which is still in force. It reasserts in Article XI. the first clause of Article XXI. of the former constitution, that the Roman Catholic Church is the religion of the state, and entitled to the support of the nation. But the next clause extends the religious liberty granted to foreign residents to *all non-Catholics*, in these words: " No person shall be molested in the territory of Spain for his religious opinions, nor for the exercise of his particular religious worship, saving the respect due to Christian morality." Very good as far as it goes. But this concession is weakened and almost neutralized by the addition: " Nevertheless, no other ceremonies, nor manifestations in public will be permitted than those of the religion of the state." [1] Thus the Constitution of 1876 restricts the liberty of non-Catholic worship to private houses. No church or chapel looking like a house of God, no tower, no bell, no procession, no public announcement is permitted by law, and Protestant preachers and evangelists depend altogether upon the tender mercies of the local magistrate, priests, and people.

Nevertheless they continue their work under these disadvantages, in about fifty humble places of worship in Madrid, Barcelona, Seville, and other cities where more liberality prevails than in ignorant and bigoted country districts. At the census of 1877 it was found that 60 per cent. of the adult population could not read.

---

[1] The XIth. article is a.compromise between the Romanists and the Liberals, and was adopted by a vote of 220 against 84. All amendments in favor of absolute religious uniformity and exclusiveness were voted down by 226 against 39 ; and all amendments for unqualified religious liberty were likewise voted down by 163 against 12. See Schulthess, "·Europäischer Geschichtskalender " for 1876. Nördlingen, 1877, p. 277. I quote the whole article in the original as published in " Las Novedades," Nueva York, No. 64, 19 de Julio, 1876 :

" ART. XI. *La religion católica, apostólica, romana es la del Estado. La nacion se obliga á mantener el culto y sus ministros.*

" *Nadie será molestado en el teritorio español por sus opiniones religiosas, ni por el ejercicio de su respectivo culto, salvo el respeto debido á la moral cristiana.*

" *No se permitirán, sin embargo, otras ceremonias ni manifestaciones públicas que las de la religion del Estado.*"

On the other hand the Spanish government has greatly diminished the material resources of the state church. By two decrees of the Cortes, passed July 23, 1835, and March 9, 1836, all monastic establishments were suppressed, and their property confiscated for the benefit of the nation.

Portugal knows and tolerates no other religion besides the Roman Catholic, except among foreign residents who may worship privately in their houses, but not in a church.[1]

Greece.

The kingdom of the Hellenes, which gained its independence in 1830, recognizes the Greek Orthodox Church as the state religion, but the Constitution of Oct. 29, 1864, guarantees complete toleration and liberty of worship to all other sects. There are in Greece Mohammedans, Jews, Roman Catholics, and a few Protestants. The Orthodox Church was formerly ruled by the Patriarch of Constantinople, but since 1833 it has been under the direction of a Holy Synod consisting of the Metropolitan of Athens and four archbishops and bishops.

Turkey.

Even Turkey has gradually to yield to the pressure of modern ideas and reforms. Once the terror of Europe, she lives now at the mercy of the Christian powers. She always allowed to the conquered Christian nations which she could not govern by Moslem law, nor kill or expel without ruining herself, a certain measure of self-government, and contented herself with appointing the head, and exacting tribute.

Seven non-Mohammedan creeds are thus recognized, namely: 1. Latins, Franks or Roman Catholics, mostly descendants of the Genoese and Venetian settlers; 2. Greeks; 3. Armenians; 4. Syrians and United Chaldeans; 5. Maronites, subject to the patriarch at Kanobin on Mount Lebanon

---

[1] The Constitution granted by Don Pedro IV. in 1826, with an addition in 1852, provides (according to the Spanish work on " Constituciones Vigentes," just quoted, Tom. II., 354 sq.) : " *La religion católica apostólica romana continuará siendo la religion del Reino. Todas las otras religiones serán permitidas á los etrangeros, así como su culto doméstico ó particular en casas destinadas á este fin, sin forma alguna exterior de templo.*"

and the Pope; 6. Protestants, chiefly converts from the Armenians; 7. Jews. Foreign residents enjoy extra-territorial rights under the protection of the ambassadors and consuls of their countries. American and other foreign missionaries have full freedom to labor among Christians and Jews. The more division among the Giaours the better for the Turks. But no Christian is allowed to convert a Moslem, nor is any Moslem allowed to deny his faith. The laws of the Koran punish apostasy with death.

After the Crimean war, in which France and England combined saved Turkey from the grasp of the Russian bear, Sultan Abdul-Medjid abolished the death penalty for apostasy by the " Hatti-Humáyoun," proclaimed February 18, 1856. But the fanaticism of the Moslem is stronger than the will of the Sultan.

The Treaty of Berlin, July 13, 1878, has inflicted another blow on the religious autonomy of the Sultan's government. Among its provisions are the following:

" ART. LXII. The Sublime Porte, having expressed the intention to maintain the principle of religious liberty, and give it the widest scope, the contracting parties take notice of this spontaneous declaration.

" In no part of the Ottoman Empire shall difference of religion be alleged against any person as a ground for exclusion or incapacity as regards the discharge of civil and political rights, admission to the public employments, functions, and honors, or the exercise of the various professions and industries.

" All persons shall be admitted, without distinction of religion, to give evidence before the tribunals.

" The freedom and outward exercise of all forms of worship are assured to all, and no hindrance shall be offered either to the hierarchical organizations of the various communions or to their relations with their spiritual chiefs.

" Ecclesiastics, pilgrims, and monks of all nationalities travelling in Turkey in Europe, or in Turkey in Asia, shall enjoy the same rights, advantages, and privileges.

" The right of official protection by the diplomatic and consular agents of the powers in Turkey is recognized both as regards the above-mentioned persons and their religious, charitable, and other establishments in the holy places and elsewhere."

DOCUMENTS.

DOCUMENT I.

Provisions of the United States Constitution Securing Religious Liberty, 1787.

Article VI., Section 3 :

" No religious test shall ever be required as a qualification to any office or public trust under the United States."

Amendments. Article I. :

" Congress shall make no law respecting an establishment of religion, or prohibiting the free exercise thereof ; or abridging the freedom of speech, or of the press ; or the right of the people peaceably to assemble, and to petition the government for a redress of grievances."

The Virginia Ordinance of 1787.

While the Constitutional Convention was in session at Philadelphia, the Continental Congress sitting under the Articles of Confederation passed an ordinance, July 13, 1787, "for the government of the territory of the United States northwest of the Ohio river." This territory was ceded by Virginia to the United States, and embraced the present States of Ohio, Indiana, Illinois, Michigan, and Wisconsin. The same ordinance was afterwards extended to Tennessee, Alabama, and Mississippi.

This ordinance provides for full religious liberty on the one hand, and for the cultivation of religion, morality, and education, as essential conditions of national prosperity. Among the articles which shall "forever remain unalterable," are the following :

Art. I. " No person demeaning himself in a peaceable and orderly manner, shall ever be molested on account of his mode of worship or religious sentiments in the said territory."

Art. III. " Religion, morality, and knowledge being necessary to good government and the happiness of mankind, schools and the means of education shall forever be encouraged."

DOCUMENT II.

Opinion of the U. S. Supreme Court on the Meaning of Religious Liberty, 1878.

Reynolds v. United States. Reports, vol. 98 (Boston : Little, Brown & Co., 1878), pp. 145 *sqq.*

The Supreme Court of the United States, in the case of Reynolds, a Mormon, charged with bigamy, decided in favor of the constitutionality and validity of the Congressional prohibition of polygamy in the Territories. Chief-Justice WAITE, in delivering the decision, gave the following opinion of religion and religious liberty (pp. 162 *sqq.*).

" Congress cannot pass a law for the government of the Territories which shall prohibit the free exercise of religion. The first amendment to the Constitution expressly forbids such legislation. Religious freedom is guaranteed everywhere throughout the United States, so far as congressional interference is concerned. The question to be determined is, whether the law now under consideration [prohibition of polygamy] comes within this prohibition.

" The word ' religion ' is not defined in the Constitution. We must go elsewhere, therefore, to ascertain its meaning, and nowhere more appropriately, we think, than to the history of the times in the midst of which the provision was adopted. The precise point of inquiry is, what is the religious freedom which has been guaranteed.

" Before the adoption of the Constitution, attempts were made in some of the Colonies and States to legislate not only in respect to the establishment of religion, but in respect to its doctrines and precepts as well. The people were taxed, against their will, for the support of religion, and sometimes for the support of particular sects to whose tenets they could not and did not subscribe. Punishments were prescribed for a failure to attend upon public worship, and sometimes for entertaining heretical opinions. The controversy upon this general subject was animated in many of the States, but seemed at last to culminate in Virginia. In 1784, the House of Delegates of that State, having under consideration ' a bill establishing provision for teachers of the Christian religion,' postponed it until the next session, and directed that the bill should be published and distributed, and that the people be requested ' to signify their opinion respecting the adoption of such a bill at the next session of assembly.'

" This brought out a determined opposition. Amongst others, Mr. Madison prepared a ' Memorial and Remonstrance,' which was widely circulated and signed, in which he demonstrated ' that religion, or the duty we owe the Creator,' was not within the cognizance of civil government. Semple's ' Virginia Baptists,' Appendix. At the next session the proposed bill was not only defeated, but another, ' for establishing religious freedom,' drafted by Mr. Jefferson, was passed. 1 Jeff. Works, 45 ; 2 Howison, Hist. of Va., 298. In the preamble of this act (12 Hening's Stat., 84) religious freedom is defined ; and after a recital ' that to suffer the civil magistrate to intrude his powers into the field of opinion, and to restrain the profession or propagation of principles on supposition of their ill tendency, is a dangerous fallacy which at once destroys all religious liberty,' it is declared ' that it is time enough for the rightful purposes of civil government for its officers to interfere when principles break out into overt acts against peace and good order.' In these two sentences is found the true distinction between what properly belongs to the church and what to the state.

" In a little more than a year after the passage of this statute the convention met which prepared the Constitution of the United States. Of this convention Mr. Jefferson was not a member, he being then absent as minister to France.

As soon as he saw the draft of the Constitution proposed for adoption, he, in a letter to a friend, expressed his disappointment at the absence of an express declaration insuring the freedom of religion (2 Jeff. Works, 355), but was willing to accept it as it was, trusting that the good sense and honest intentions of the people would bring about the necessary alterations.   1 Jeff. Works, 79. Five of the States, while adopting the Constitution, proposed amendments. Three, New Hampshire, New York, and Virginia, included in one form or another a declaration of religious freedom in the changes they desired to have made, as did also North Carolina, where the convention at first declined to ratify the Constitution until the proposed amendments were acted upon.   Accordingly, at the first session of the first Congress the amendment now under consideration was proposed with others by Mr. Madison.   It met the views of the advocates of religious freedom, and was adopted.   Mr. Jefferson afterwards, in reply to an address to him by a committee of the Danbury Baptist Association (8 *id.*, 113), took occasion to say : ' Believing with you that religion is a matter which lies solely between man and his God ; that he owes account to none other for his faith or his worship ; that the legislative powers of the government reach actions only, and not opinions,—I contemplate with sovereign reverence that act of the whole American people which declared that their legislature should ' make no law respecting an establishment of religion or prohibiting the free exercise thereof,' thus building a wall of separation between church and state. Adhering to this expression of the supreme will of the nation in behalf of the rights of conscience, I shall see with sincere satisfaction the progress of those sentiments which tend to restore man to all his natural rights, convinced he has no natural right in opposition to his social duties.'

" Coming as this does from an acknowledged leader of the advocates of the measure, it may be accepted almost as an authoritative declaration of the scope and effect of the amendment thus secured. Congress was deprived of all legislative power over mere opinion, but was left free to reach actions which were in violation of social duties or subversive of good order.

" Polygamy has always been odious among the northern and western nations of Europe, and, until the establishment of the Mormon Church, was almost exclusively a feature of the life of Asiatic and of African people.   At common law, the second marriage was always void (2 Kent, Com., 79), and from the earliest history of England polygamy has been treated as an offence against society. After the establishment of the ecclesiastical courts, and until the time of James I., it was punished through the instrumentality of those tribunals, not merely because ecclesiastical rights had been violated, but because upon the separation of the ecclesiastical courts from the civil the ecclesiastical were supposed to be the most appropriate for the trial of matrimonial causes and offences against the rights of marriage, just as they were for testamentary causes and the settlement of the estates of deceased persons.

" By the statute of I. James I. (c. 11), the offence, if committed in England or Wales, was made punishable in the civil courts, and the penalty was death. As this statute was limited in its operation to England and Wales, it was at a very early period re-enacted, generally with some modifications, in all the colonies.   In connection with the case we are now considering, it is a significant fact that on the 8th of December, 1788, after the passage of the act establishing religious freedom, and after the convention of Virginia had recommended as an amendment to the Constitution of the United States the declaration in a bill of rights that ' all men have an equal, natural, and unalienable right to the free exercise of religion, according to the dictates of conscience,' the legislature of that State substantially enacted the statute of James I., death penalty included, because, as recited in the preamble, ' it hath been doubted whether bigamy or polygamy be punishable by the laws of this Commonwealth.' 12 Hening's Stat., 691. From that day to this we think it may safely be said there never has been a time in any State of the Union when polygamy has not been an offence against society, cognizable by the civil courts, and punishable with more or less severity. In the face of all this evidence, it is impossible to believe that the constitutional guaranty of religious freedom was intended to prohibit legislation in respect to this most important feature of social life. Marriage, while from its very nature a sacred obligation, is nevertheless, in most civilized nations, a civil contract, and usually regulated by law. Upon it society may be said to be built, and out of its fruits spring social relations and social obligations and duties, with which government is necessarily required to deal. In fact, according as monogamous or polygamous marriages are allowed, do we find the principles on which the government of the people, to a greater or less extent, rests. Professor Lieber says, polygamy leads to the patriarchal principle, and when applied to large communities, fetters the people in stationary despotism, while that principle cannot long exist in connection with monogamy. Chancellor Kent observes that this remark is equally striking and profound. 2 Kent, Com., 81, note (e). An exceptional colony of polygamists under an exceptional leadership may sometimes exist for a time without appearing to disturb the social condition of the people who surround it ; but there cannot be a doubt that, unless restricted by some form of constitution, it is within the legitimate scope of the power of every civil government to determine whether polygamy or monogamy shall be the law of social life under its dominion.

" In our opinion the statute immediately under consideration is within the legislative power of Congress. It is constitutional and valid as prescribing a rule of action for all those residing in the Territories, and in places over which the United States have exclusive control. This being so, the only question which remains is whether those who make polygamy a part of their religion are excepted from the operation of the statute. If they are, then those who do not make polygamy a part of their religious belief may be found guilty and punished, while those who do must.be acquitted and go free. This would be introducing a new element into criminal law. Laws are made for the government of actions, and while they cannot interfere with mere religious belief and opinions, they may with practices. Suppose one believed that human sacrifices were a necessary part of religious worship, would it be seriously contended that the civil government under which he lived could not interfere to prevent a sacrifice ? Or, if a wife religiously believed it was her duty to burn herself upon the funeral pile of her dead husband, would it be beyond the power of the civil government to prevent her carrying her belief into practice ?

"So here, as a law of the organization of society under the exclusive dominion of the United States, it is provided that plural marriages shall not be allowed. Can a man excuse his practices to the contrary because of his religious belief? To permit this would be to make the professed doctrines of religious belief superior to the law of the land, and in effect to permit every citizen to become a law unto himself. Government would exist only in name under such circumstances."

DOCUMENT III.

Dr. Franklin's Speech in Support of his Motion for Prayers in the Federal Convention.

From Madison's Report in "The Madison Papers," vol. ii. 984-986 ; reprinted in Elliot's "Debates," enlarged edition, vol. v. pp. 253-255.

"Dr. FRANKLIN : Mr. President, the small progress we have made after four or five weeks' close attendance and continual reasoning with each other—our different sentiments on almost every question, several of the last producing as many noes as ayes—is, methinks, a melancholy proof of the imperfection of the human understanding. We indeed seem to feel our own want of political wisdom, since we have been running about in search of it. We have gone back to ancient history for models of government, and examined the different forms of those republics which, having been formed with the seeds of their own dissolution, no longer exist. And we have viewed modern States all round Europe, but find none of their constitutions suitable to our circumstances.

"In this situation of this assembly, as it were, in the dark, to find political truth, and scarce able to distinguish it when presented to us, how has it happened, sir, that we have not hitherto once thought of humbly applying to the Father of lights to illuminate our understandings? In the beginning of the contest with Great Britain, when we were sensible of danger, we had daily prayer in this room for the divine protection. Our prayers, sir, were heard, and they were graciously answered. All of us who were engaged in the struggle must have observed frequent instances of a superintending Providence in our favor. To that kind Providence we owe this happy opportunity of consulting in peace on the means of establishing our future national felicity. And have we now forgotten that powerful Friend? Or do we imagine that we no longer need his assistance?

"I have lived, sir, a long time, and, the longer I live, the more convincing proofs I see of this truth—that God governs in the affairs of men. And if a sparrow cannot fall to the ground without his notice, is it possible that an empire can rise without his aid? We have been assured, sir, in the sacred writings that 'except the Lord build the house, they labor in vain that build it.' I firmly believe this ; and I also believe that without his concurring aid we shall succeed, in this political building, no better than the builders of Babel. We shall be divided by our little partial local interests ; our projects will be confounded ; and we ourselves shall become a reproach and by-word down to future ages. And what is worse, mankind may hereafter, from this unfortunate instance, despair of establishing governments by human wisdom, and leave it to chance, war, and conquest.

" I therefore beg to move that henceforth prayers, imploring the assistance of heaven and its blessings on our deliberations, be held in this assembly every morning before we proceed to business, and that one or more of the clergy of this city be requested to officiate in that service."

" Mr. SHERMAN seconded the motion.

" Mr. HAMILTON, and several others, expressed their apprehensions that, however proper such a resolution might have been at the beginning of the Convention, it might at this late day, in the first place, bring on it some disagreeable animadversions ; and, in the second, lead the public to believe that the embarrassments and dissensions within the Convention had suggested this measure.

" It was answered by Dr. FRANKLIN, Mr. SHERMAN, and others, that the past omission of a duty could not justify a further omission ; that the rejection of such a proposition would expose the Convention to more unpleasant animad versions than the adoption of it ; and that the alarm out of doors that might be excited for the state of things within, would at least be as likely to do good as ill.

" Mr. WILLIAMSON observed that the true cause of the omission could not be mistaken. The Convention had no funds.

" Mr. RANDOLPH proposed, in order to give a favorable aspect to the measure, that a sermon be preached at the request of the Convention on the Fourth of July, the anniversary of Independence ; and thenceforward prayers, etc., to be read in the Convention every morning.

" Dr. FRANKLIN seconded this motion. After several unsuccessful attempts for silently postponing this matter by adjourning, the adjournment was at length carried, without any vote on the motion."

The speech of Dr. Franklin was written and read to the Convention by his colleague, Mr. Wilson, "it being inconvenient to the Doctor to remain long on his feet." See Madison, in the introduction to his report of the Debates, Elliot, vol. v., 122.

The motion was not voted on and virtually withdrawn. In the " Works of Benjamin Franklin," edited by Jared Sparks, Boston, 1847, vol. v., p. 153, the speech of Dr. Franklin is given, with the following note of his on p. 155 : " The Convention, except three or four persons, thought prayers unnecessary ! " The remarks of Hamilton and others, however, show that they were not opposed to prayers, but to the untimeliness of the motion.

At the enthusiastic centennial celebration of the Constitution in Philadelphia, September 17, 1887, prayer was not neglected. Bishop Potter, of New York, made the opening, Cardinal Gibbons, of Baltimore, the closing prayer, and both prelates performed the solemn duty with excellent taste, falling back upon the common ground of Protestant and Catholic Christianity. The Rev. Dr. Witherspoon, a Presbyterian clergyman, pronounced the benediction. President Cleveland embodied Franklin's speech in his eulogy of the Constitution.

James Madison, in a letter to Mr. Sparks, dated Montpellier, April 8, 1831 (Elliot's " Debates," vol. i., p. 508, revised ed.), makes the following allusion to Franklin's motion : " It was during that period of gloom [the hot controversy between the larger and smaller States on the rule of voting in the Senate] that Dr. Franklin made the proposition for a religious service in the Convention, an account of which was so erroneously given, with every semblance of authenticity, through the *National Intelligencer*, several years ago."

DOCUMENT IV.

Acts of Congress in regard to the Bible.

1. Act of the Continental Congress, Sept. 11, 1777.

From " Journal of Congress, Containing the Proceedings from January 1st, 1777, to January 1st, 1778. Published by order of Congress," vol. iii., Philadelphia (John Dunlap), pp. 383–386.

" The committee to whom the memorial of Doctor Allison[1] and others was referred, report, ' That they have conferred fully with the printers, etc., in this city, and are of the opinion, that the proper types for printing the Bible are not to be had in this country, and that the paper cannot be procured, but with such difficulties and subject to such casualties as render any dependence on it altogether improper ; that to import types for the purpose of setting up an entire edition of the Bible, and to strike off 30,000 copies, with paper, binding, etc., will cost 10,272 *l.* 10 *s.* 0 *d.*, which must be advanced by Congress to be reimbursed by the sale of the books ; that in the opinion of the committee, considerable difficulties will attend the procuring the types and paper ; that afterwards the risque of importing them will considerably enhance the cost, and that the calculations are subject to such uncertainty in the present state of affairs, that Congress cannot much rely on them ; that the use of the Bible is so universal, and its importance so great, that your committee refer the above to the consideration of Congress, and if Congress shall not think it expedient to order the importation of types and paper, the committee recommend that Congress will order the committee of commerce to import 20,000 Bibles from Holland, Scotland or elsewhere into the different ports of the States of the Union.'

" Whereupon it was moved, That the committee of commerce be directed to import 20,000 copies of the Bible.

New Hampshire.—Mr. Folsom, ay ; Mr. Frost, ay—ay.

Massachusetts Bay.—Mr. S. Adams, ay ; Mr. J. Adams, ay ; Mr. Gerry, ay ; Mr. Lovell, ay—ay.

Rhode Island.—Mr. Marchant, ay—ay.

Connecticut.—Mr. Dyer, ay ; Mr. Law, ay ; Mr. Williams, ay—ay.

New York.—Mr. Duane, no—*

New Jersey.—Mr Witherspoon, ay ; Mr. Clarke, ay—ay.

Pennsylvania.—Mr. Wilson, ay ; Mr. Roberdeau, ay—ay.

Delaware.—Mr. Reed, no—no.

Maryland.—Mr. Chase, no—*

Virginia.—Mr. Harrison, no ; Mr. F. L. Lee, ay ; Mr. Jones, no—no.

---

[1] Dr. Patrick Allison was one of the two chaplains of the Continental Congress, the Rev. William White (afterwards Bishop of the diocese of Pennsylvania) being the other. The memorial referred to was a petition to Congress to issue an edition of the Bible, under the direction and at the expense of the government.—P. S.

North Carolina.—Mr. Harnett, no—no.
South Carolina.—Mr. Middleton, no ; Mr. Heyward, no ; Mr. Laurens, ay—no.
Georgia.—Mr. Brownson, ay—ay.
" So it was resolved in the affirmative."

2. Act of the Continental Congress, passed September 12, 1782.
From " Journal of Congress and of the United States in Congress Assembled," vol. vii., Philad. (D. C. Claypoole), pp. 468, 469.

" The committee, consisting of Mr. Duane, Mr. M'Keen and Mr. Witherspoon, to whom was referred a memorial of Robert Aitkin,[1] printer, dated
January 21st, 1781, respecting an edition of the Holy Scriptures, report :
" ' That Mr. Aitkin [1] has, at a great expense, now finished an American
edition of the Holy Scriptures in English ; that the committee have, from time
to time, attended to his progress in the work ; that they also recommend it to
the two Chaplains of Congress to examine and give their opinion of the execution, who have accordingly reported thereof.
" ' The recommendation and the report being as follows :

" ' PHILADELPHIA, September 1st, 1782.
" ' REVEREND GENTLEMEN :—Our knowledge of your piety and public spirit
leads us without apology to recommend to your particular attention the edition
of the Holy Scriptures publishing by Mr. Aitkin. He undertook this expen-
sive work at a time, when from the circumstances of the war, an English
edition of the Bible could not be imported, nor any opinion formed how long
the obstruction might continue. On this account particularly he deserves
applause and encouragement. We therefore wish you, Reverend gentlemen,
to examine the execution of the work, and if approved, to give it the sanction
of your judgment and the weight of your recommendation.
" ' We are, with very great respect, your most obedient servants,
" ' (Signed)   JAMES DUANE, Chairman,
" ' In behalf of a committee of Congress on Mr. Aitkin's memorial.

" ' Reverend Dr. White and Reverend Mr. Duffield,
         Chaplains of the United States assembled.'

" ' *Report.*

" ' GENTLEMEN :
" ' Agreeably to your desire, we have paid attention to Mr. Robert Aitkin's
impression of the Holy Scriptures of the Old and New Testament. Having
selected and examined a variety of new passages throughout the work, we
are of opinion that it is executed with great accuracy as to the sense, and with
as few grammatical and typographical errors as could be expected in an undertaking of such magnitude. Being ourselves witnesses of the demand for this
invaluable book, we rejoice in the present prospect of a supply, hoping that it
will prove as advantageous as it is honorable to the gentleman, who has ex-

---

[1] A misprint for Aitken.—P. S.

erted himself to furnish it at the evident risque of private fortune. We are, gentlemen, your very respectful and humble servants,

" ' (Signed)　　**WILLIAM WHITE,**

" ' **GEORGE DUFFIELD.**

" ' Honorable James Duane, Esquire, Chairman,
　　and the other honorable gentlemen of the
　　committee of Congress on Mr. Aitkin's
　　memorial.

" ' PHILADELPHIA, September 10th, 1782.'

" Whereupon,

" *Resolved*, That the United States, in Congress assembled, highly approve the pious and laudable undertaking of Mr. Aitkin, as subservient to the interest of religion, as well as an instance of the progress of arts in this country, and being satisfied from the above report of his care and accuracy in the execution of the work, they recommend this edition of the Bible to the inhabitants of the United States, and hereby authorize him to publish this recommendation in the manner he shall think proper."

3. Joint Resolution in behalf of the American Company [Committee][1] of Revisers of the New Testament for Return and Remission of Duties.

" *Whereas*, 2,100 copies of the book known as the Revision of the New Testament of our Lord and Saviour Jesus Christ, printed by the University Presses of Oxford and Cambridge in England, being the joint and gratuitous work of two companies of translators, one in England and the other in the United States, were sent, under the direction of the English Company of Revisers, to and for the use and distribution of the American Company of Revisers, and were heretofore imported at the Port of New York, for or in behalf of the American Company of Revisers, and the duties paid thereon ; and

" *Whereas*, The revision of the translation of the Old Testament Scriptures is now progressing under similar auspices, and the same is to be printed in a similar manner, and copies of them will be required for the use and distribution of the American Company of Revisers, therefore,

" *Be it Resolved*, By the Senate and House of Representatives of the United States of America, in Congress assembled, That the Secretary of the Treasury be and is hereby authorized and directed to ascertain the facts of such past and expected importations of the revisions of the Bible, and if he shall be satisfied that they are substantially as above stated, then to refund and repay, out of any moneys in the Treasury not otherwise appropriated, to the American Company of Revisers, of which Reverend Doctor Philip Schaff, of New York, is Chairman,[2] and Reverend Doctor Henry Day, of New York,[3] is Secretary, through and by said officers, the amount of duties heretofore paid upon the said books so imported ; and that he be, and further is, authorized and directed

---

[1] There were two committees on revision, one for England and one for America ; each committee was composed of two companies, one for the Old and one for the New Testament.—P. S.

[2] President of the committee ; the title Chairman being given to the presiding officers of the two separate companies (Dr. Woolsey and Dr. Green).—P. S.

[3] A mistake for Rev. Dr. George E. Day, of New Haven.—P. S.

to remit the duties upon, and to admit to entry free of duty or custom, the books containing the revision of the Old Testament which may be hereafter imported from England by or on behalf of the American Company of Revisers, for their use and distribution as above set forth,

"*Provided*, that future importations of the Bible for the purposes set forth in this Act shall not exceed two thousand copies.

"Approved, March 11, 1882."

DOCUMENT V.

Judge Story's Explanation of the Constitutional Guarantee of Religious Liberty.

Judge JOSEPH STORY, the authoritative expounder of the American Constitution, explains the third section of Article VI., and the First Amendment of the Constitution ("Commentaries on the Constitution of the United States," Boston, 1833, pp. 690 *sq.*, and 698–703) as follows :

"This clause [the last in Art. VI., § 3] is not introduced merely for the purpose of satisfying the scruples of many respectable persons who feel an invincible repugnance to any religious test or affirmation. It had a higher object : to cut off forever every pretense of any alliance between church and state in the national government. The framers of the constitution were fully sensible of the dangers from this source, marked out in the history of other ages and countries, and not wholly unknown to our own. They knew that bigotry was unceasingly vigilant in its stratagems to secure to itself an exclusive ascendency over the human mind, and that intolerance was ever ready to arm itself with all the terrors of the civil power to exterminate those who doubted its dogmas or resisted its infallibility. The Catholic and Protestant had alternately waged the most ferocious and unrelenting warfare on each other, and Protestantism, at the very moment when it was proclaiming the right of private judgment, prescribed boundaries to that right, beyond which if any one dared to pass he must seal his rashness with the blood of martyrdom. The history of the parent country, too, could not fail to instruct them in the uses and the abuses of religious tests. They there found the pains and penalties of nonconformity written in no equivocal language, and enforced with a stern and vindictive jealousy. . . .

"The right of society or government to interfere in matters of religion will hardly be contested by any persons who believe that piety, religion, and morality are intimately connected with the well-being of the state, and indispensable to the administration of civil justice. The promulgation of the great doctrines of religion ; the being, and attributes, and providence of one almighty God ; the responsibility to him for all our actions, founded upon moral freedom and accountability ; a future state of rewards and punishments ; the cultivation of all the personal, social, and benevolent virtues ;—these never can be a matter of indifference in any well-ordered community. It is, indeed, difficult to conceive how any civilized society can well exist without them, And, at all events, it is impossible for those who believe in the truth of Christianity, as a divine revelation, to doubt that it is the especial duty of government to foster and encourage it among all the citizens and subjects. This is a point wholly distinct from that of the right of private judgment in matters of religion, and of the freedom of public worship according to the dictates of one's own conscience.

" The real difficulty lies in ascertaining the limits to which government may rightfully go in fostering and encouraging religion. Three cases may easily be supposed. One, where a government affords aid to a particular religion, leaving all persons free to adopt any other ; another, where it creates an ecclesiastical establishment for the propagation of the doctrines of a particular sect of that religion, leaving a like freedom to all others ; and, a third, where it creates such an establishment, and excludes all persons not belonging to it, either wholly or in part, from any participation in the public honors, trusts, emoluments, privileges, and immunities of the state. For instance, a government may simply declare that the Christian religion shall be the religion of the state, and shall be aided and encouraged in all the varieties of sects belonging to it ; or it may declare that the Catholic or the Protestant religion shall be the religion of the state, leaving every man to the free enjoyment of his own religious opinions ; or it may establish the doctrines of a particular sect, as of Episcopalians, as the religion of the state, with a like freedom ; or it may establish the doctrines of a particular sect as exclusively the religion of the state, tolerating others to a limited extent, or excluding all not belonging to it from all public honors, trusts, emoluments, privileges, and immunities.

" Probably at the time of the adoption of the constitution, and of the amendment to it now under consideration, the general, if not the universal, sentiment in America was that Christianity ought to receive encouragement from the state, so far as it is not incompatible with the private rights of conscience and the freedom of religious worship. An attempt to level all religions, and to make it a matter of state policy to hold all in utter indifference, would have created universal disapprobation, if not universal indignation.

" It yet remains a problem to be solved in human affairs whether any free government can be permanent where the public worship of God and the support of religion constitute no part of the policy or duty of the state in any assignable shape. The future experience of Christendom, and chiefly of the American States, must settle this problem, as yet new in the history of the world, abundant as it has been in experiments in the theory of government.

" But the duty of supporting religion, and especially the Christian religion, is very different from the right to force the consciences of other men, or to punish them for worshipping God in the manner which they believe their accountability to him requires. It has been truly said that ' religion, or the duty we owe to our Creator, and the manner of discharging it, can be dictated only by reason and conviction, not by force or violence.' Mr. Locke himself, who did not doubt the right of government to interfere in matters of religion, and especially to encourage Christianity, has at the same time expressed his opinion of the right of private judgment and liberty of conscience in a manner becoming his character as a sincere friend of civil and religious liberty. ' No man or society of men,' says he, ' have any authority to impose their opinions or interpretations on any other, the meanest Christian ; since, in matters of religion, every man must know, and believe, and give an account for himself.' The rights of conscience are, indeed, beyond the just reach of any human power.

They are given by God, and cannot be encroached upon by human authority without a criminal disobedience of the precepts of natural, as well as revealed, religion.

" The real object of the amendment was not to countenance, much less to advance, Mahometanism, or Judaism, or infidelity, by prostrating Christianity ; but to exclude all rivalry among Christian sects, and to prevent any national ecclesiastical establishment which should give to an hierarchy the exclusive patronage of the national government. It thus sought to cut off the means of religious persecution (the vice and pest of former ages), and the power of subverting the rights of conscience in matters of religion, which had been trampled upon almost from the days of the Apostles to the present age. The history of the parent country had afforded the most solemn warnings and melancholy instructions on this head ; and even New England, the land of the persecuted Puritans, as well as other colonies, where the Church of England had maintained its superiority, had furnished a chapter as full of dark bigotry and intolerance as any which could be found to disgrace the pages of foreign annals. Apostasy, heresy, and nonconformity have been standard crimes for public appeals to kindle the flames of persecution and apologize for the most atrocious triumphs over innocence and virtue.

" It was under a solemn consciousness of the dangers from ecclesiastical ambition, the bigotry of spiritual pride, and the intolerance of sects, thus exemplified in our domestic as well as in our foreign annals, that it was deemed advisable to exclude from the national government all power to act upon the subject. The situation, too, of the different states equally proclaimed the policy as well as the necessity of such an exclusion. In some of the States, Episcopalians constituted the predominant sect ; in others, Presbyterians ; in others, Congregationalists ; in others, Quakers ; and in others again there was a close numerical rivalry among contending sects. It was impossible that there should not arise perpetual strife and perpetual jealousy on the subject of ecclesiastical ascendancy if the national government were left free to create a religious establishment. The only security was in extirpating the power. But this alone would have been an imperfect security, if it had not been followed up by a declaration of the right of the free exercise of religion, and a prohibition (as we have seen) of all religious tests. Thus, the whole power over the subject of religion is left exclusively to the State governments, to be acted upon according to their own sense of justice and the State constitutions ; and the Catholic and the Protestant, the Calvinist and the Arminian, the Jew and the Infidel, may sit down at the common table of the national councils without any inquisition into their faith or mode of worship."

DOCUMENT VI.

Opinion of Dr. Francis Lieber on Religious Liberty.

From " Civil Liberty and Self-Government," by Francis Lieber, LL.D. Philadelphia, 1859, p. 99.

" Liberty of conscience, or, as it ought to be called more properly,[1] the liberty

[1] Conscience lies beyond the reach of government. " Thoughts are free," is an old German saying. The same must be said of feelings and conscience. That which government, even the most despotic, can alone interfere with, is the profession of religion, worship, and church government.

of worship, is one of the primordial rights of man, and no system of liberty can be considered comprehensive which does not include guarantees for the free exercise of this right. It belongs to American liberty to separate entirely the institution which has for its object the support and diffusion of religion from the political government. We have seen already what our constitution says on this point. All state constitutions have similar provisions. They prohibit government from founding or endowing churches, and from demanding a religious qualification for any office or the exercise of any right. They are not hostile to religion, for we see that all the State governments direct or allow the Bible to be read in the public schools ; but they adhere strictly to these two points : No worship shall be interfered with, either directly by persecution, or indirectly by disqualifying members of certain sects, or by favoring one sect above the others ; and no church shall be declared the church of the state, or ' established church ' ; nor shall the people be taxed by government to support the clergy of all the churches, as is the case in France."

DOCUMENT VII.

Judge Cooley on Religious Liberty in the United States.

JUDGE THOMAS M. COOLEY, in his "Constitutional Limitations" (Little, Brown & Co., Boston, 5th ed. 1883), pp. 576 *sqq.*, has the following chapter :

"OF RELIGIOUS LIBERTY.

"A careful examination of the American constitutions will disclose the fact that nothing is more fully set forth or more plainly expressed than the determination of their authors to preserve and perpetuate religious liberty and to guard against the slightest approach towards the establishment of an inequality in the civil and political rights of citizens, which shall have for its basis only their differences of religious belief. The American people came to the work of framing their fundamental laws, after centuries of religious oppression and persecution, sometimes by one party or sect and sometimes by another, had taught them the utter futility of all attempts to propagate religious opinions by the rewards, penalties, or terrors of human laws. They could not fail to perceive, also, that a union of church and state, like that which existed in England, if not wholly impracticable in America, was certainly opposed to the spirit of our institutions, and that any domineering of one sect over another was repressing to the energies of the people, and must necessarily tend to discontent and disorder. Whatever, therefore, may have been their individual sentiments upon religious questions, or upon the propriety of the state assuming supervision and control of religious affairs under other circumstances, the general voice has been, that persons of every religious persuasion should be made equal before the law, and that questions of religious belief and religious worship should be questions between each individual man and his Maker. Of these questions human tribunals, so long as the public order is not disturbed, are not to take cognizance, except as the individual, by his voluntary action in associating himself with a religious organization, may have conferred upon such organization a jurisdiction over him in ecclesiastical matters. These constitutions, therefore, have not established religious toleration merely, but religious equality, in that particular being far in advance not only of the mother country, but also of much of the colonial legislation, which, though more liberal than that of other civilized countries, nevertheless, exhibited features of discrimination based upon religious beliefs or professions.

" Considerable differences will appear in the provisions in the State constitutions on the general subject of the present chapter, some of them being confined to declarations and prohibitions whose purpose is to secure the most perfect equality before the law of all shades of religious belief, while some exhibit a jealousy of ecclesiastical authority by making persons who exercise the functions of clergyman, priest, or teacher of any religious persuasion, society, or sect, ineligible to civil office ; and still others show some traces of the old notion that truth and a sense of duty do not consort with skepticism in religion. There are exceptional clauses, however, though not many in number ; and it is believed that where they exist they are not often made use of to deprive any person of the civil or political rights or privileges which are placed by law within the reach of his fellows.

" Those things which are not lawful under any of the American constitutions may be stated thus :

" I. Any law respecting an establishment of religion. The legislatures have not been left at liberty to effect a union of church and state, or to establish preferences by law in favor of any one religious persuasion or mode of worship. There is not complete religious liberty where any one sect is favored by the state and given an advantage by law over other sects. Whatever establishes a distinction against one class or sect, is, to the extent to which the distinction operates unfavorably, a persecution ; and if based on religious grounds, a religious persecution. The extent of the discrimination is not material to the principle. It is enough that it creates an inequality of right or privilege.

" II. Compulsory support, by taxation or otherwise, of religious instruction. Not only is no one denomination to be favored at the expense of the rest, but all support of religious instruction must be entirely voluntary. It is not within the sphere of government to coerce it.

" III. Compulsory attendance upon religious worship. Whoever is not led by choice or a sense of duty to attend upon the ordinances of religion is not to be compelled to do so by the state. It is the province of the state to enforce, so far as it may be found practicable, the obligations and duties which the citizen may be under or may owe to his fellow-citizen or to society ; but those which spring from the relations between himself and his Maker are to be enforced by the admonitions of the conscience, and not by the penalties of human laws. Indeed, as all real worship must essentially and necessarily consist in the free-will offering of adoration and gratitude by the creature to the Creator, human laws are obviously inadequate to incite or compel those internal and voluntary emotions which shall induce it ; and human penalties at most could only enforce the observance of idle ceremonies which, when unwillingly performed, are alike valueless to the participants, and devoid of all the elements of true worship.

"IV. Restraints upon the free exercise of religion according to the dictates of the conscience. No external authority is to place itself between the finite being and the Infinite, when the former is seeking to render the homage that is due, and in a mode which commends itself to his conscience and judgment as being suitable for him to render and acceptable to its object.

"V. Restraints upon the expression of religious belief. An earnest believer usually regards it as his duty to propagate his opinions and to bring others to his views. To deprive him of this right is to take from him the power to perform what he considers a most sacred obligation.

"These are the prohibitions which in some form of words are to be found in the American constitutions, and which secure freedom of conscience and of religious worship. No man, in religious matters, is to be subjected to the censorship of the state or of any public authority; and the state is not to inquire into or take notice of religious belief when the citizen performs his duty to the state and to his fellows, and is guilty of no breach of public morals or public decorum.

"But while thus careful to establish, protect, and defend religious freedom and equality, the American constitutions contain no provisions which prohibit the authorities from such solemn recognition of a superintending Providence in public transactions and exercises as the general religious sentiment of mankind inspires, and as seems meet and proper in finite and dependent beings. Whatever may be the shades of religious belief, all must acknowledge the fitness of recognizing in important human affairs the superintending care and control of the great Governor of the Universe, and of acknowledging with thanksgiving His boundless favors, or bowing in contrition when visited with the penalties of His broken laws. No principle of constitutional law is violated when thanksgiving or fast days are appointed; when chaplains are designated for the army and navy; when legislative sessions are opened with prayer or the reading of the Scriptures, or when religious teaching is encouraged by a general exemption of the houses of religious worship from taxation for the support of the state government. Undoubtedly the spirit of the constitution will require, in all these cases, that care be taken to avoid discrimination in favor of or against any one religious denomination or sect; but the power to do any of these things does not become unconstitutional simply because of its susceptibility to abuse. This public recognition of religious worship, however, is not based entirely, perhaps not even mainly, upon a sense of what is due to the Supreme Being himself as the author of all good and of all law; but the same reasons of state policy which induce the government to aid institutions of charity and seminaries of instruction will incline it also to foster religious worship and religious institutions as conservators of the public morals, and valuable, if not indispensable, assistants in the preservation of the public order.

"Nor, while recognizing a superintending Providence, are we always precluded from recognizing, also, in the rules prescribed for the conduct of the citizen, the notorious fact that the prevailing religion in the States is Christian. Some acts would be offensive to public sentiment in a Christian community, and would tend to public disorder, which in a Mohammedan or Pagan country might be passed by without notice, or even be regarded as meritorious ; just as some things would be considered indecent and worthy of reprobation and punishment as such in one state of society, which in another would be in accord with the prevailing customs, and therefore defended and protected by the laws. The criminal laws of every country are shaped in greater or less degree by the prevailing public sentiment as to what is right, proper, and decorous, or the reverse ; and they punish those acts as crimes which disturb the peace and order, or tend to shock the moral sense or sense of propriety and decency of the community. The moral sense is largely regulated and controlled by the religious belief ; and therefore it is that those things which, estimated by a Christian standard, are profane and blasphemous, are properly punished as crimes against society, since they are offensive in the highest degree to the general public sense, and have a direct tendency to undermine the moral support of the laws and to corrupt the community.

" It is frequently said that Christianity is a part of the law of the land. In a certain sense and for certain purposes this is true. The best features of the common law, and especially those which regard the family and social relations ; which compel the parent to support the child, the husband to support the wife ; which make the marriage-tie permanent and forbid polygamy,—if not derived from, have at least been improved and strengthened by the prevailing religion and the teachings of its sacred Book. But the law does not attempt to enforce the precepts of Christianity on the ground of their sacred character or divine origin. Some of those precepts, though we may admit their continual and universal obligation, we must nevertheless recognize as being incapable of enforcement by human laws. That standard of morality which requires one to love his neighbor as himself, we must admit is too elevated to be accepted by human tribunals as the proper test by which to judge the conduct of the citizen ; and one could hardly be held responsible to the criminal laws if in goodness of heart and spontaneous charity he fell something short of the Good Samaritan. The precepts of Christianity, moreover, affect the heart, and address themselves to the conscience, while the laws of the state can regard the outward conduct only ; and for these several reasons Christianity is not a part of the law of the land in any sense which entitles the courts to take notice of and base their judgments upon it, except so far as they can find that its precepts and principles have been incorporated in and made a component part of the positive law of the state.

" Mr. Justice STORY has said in the Girard Will case that, although Christianity is a part of the common law of the state, it is only so in this qualified sense, that *its divine origin and truth are admitted*, and therefore it is not to be maliciously and openly reviled and blasphemed against, to the annoyance of believers or to the injury of the public. It may be doubted, however, if the punishment of blasphemy is based necessarily upon an admission of the divine origin or truth of the Christian religion, or incapable of being otherwise justified.

" Blasphemy has been defined as consisting in speaking evil of the Deity, with an impious purpose to derogate from the divine majesty, and to alienate the minds of others from the love and reverence of God. It is purposely using words concerning the Supreme Being calculated and designed to impair and destroy the reverence, respect, and confidence due to Him, as the intelligent Creator, Governor, and Judge of the world. It embraces the idea of detraction as regards the character and attributes of God, as calumny usually carries the same idea when applied to an individual. It is a wilful and malicious attempt to lessen men's reverence of God, by denying his existence or his attributes as an intelligent Creator, Governor, and Judge of men, and to prevent their having confidence in Him as such. Contumelious reproaches and profane ridicule of Christ or of the Holy Scriptures have the same evil effect in sapping the foundations of society and of public order, and are classed under the same head.

" In an early case where a prosecution for blasphemy came before Lord HALE, he is reported to have said : ' Such kind of wicked, blasphemous words are not only an offence to God and religion, but a crime against the laws, state, and government, and therefore punishable in the Court of King's Bench. For to say religion is a cheat, is to subvert all those obligations whereby civil society is preserved ; that Christianity is a part of the laws of England, and to reproach the Christian religion is to speak in subversion of the law.' Eminent judges in this country have adopted this language, and applied it to prosecutions for blasphemy, where the charge consisted in malicious ridicule of the author and founder of the Christian religion. The early cases in New York and Massachusetts are particularly marked by clearness and precision on this point, and Mr. Justice CLAYTON, of Delaware, has also adopted and followed the ruling of Lord Chief-Justice HALE, with such explanations of the true basis and justification of these prosecutions as to give us a clear understanding of the maxim that Christianity is a part of the law of the land, as understood and applied by the courts in these cases. Taken with the explanation given, there is nothing in the maxim of which the believer in any creed, or the disbeliever of all, can justly complain. The language which the Christian regards as blasphemous, no man in sound mind can feel under a sense of duty to make use of under any circumstances, and no person is therefore deprived of a right when he is prohibited, under penalties, from uttering it.

" But it does not follow because blasphemy is punishable as a crime, that therefore one is not at liberty to dispute and argue against the truth of the Christian religion, or of any accepted dogma. Its ' divine origin and truth ' are not so far admitted in the law as to preclude their being controverted. To forbid discussion on this subject, except by the various sects of believers, would be to abridge the liberty of speech and of the press in a point which, with many, would be regarded as most important of all. Blasphemy implies something more than a denial of any of the truths of religion, even of the highest and most vital. A bad motive must exist ; there must be a wilful and malicious attempt to lessen men's reverence for the Deity, or for the accepted religion. But outside of such wilful and malicious attempt, there is a broad field for candid investigation and discussion, which is as much open to the Jew and the Mohammedan as to the professors of the Christian faith. ' No author or printer who fairly and conscientiously promulgates the opinions with whose truths he is impressed, for the benefit of others, is answerable as a criminal.

A malicious and mischievous intention is, in such a case, the broad boundary between right and wrong ; it is to be collected from the offensive levity, scurrilous and opprobrious language, and other circumstances, whether the act of the party was malicious.' Legal blasphemy implies that the words were uttered in a wanton manner, ' with a wicked and malicious disposition, and not in a serious discussion upon any controverted point in religion.' The courts have always been careful, in administering the law, to say that they did not intend to include in blasphemy disputes between learned men upon particular controverted points. The constitutional provisions for the protection of religious liberty not only include within their protecting power all sentiments and professions concerning or upon the subject of religion, but they guarantee to every one a perfect right to form and promulgate such opinions and doctrines upon religious matters, and in relation to the existence, power, attributes, and providence of a Supreme Being as to himself shall seem reasonable and correct. In doing this he acts under an awful responsibility, but it is not to any human tribunal.

" Other forms of profanity besides that of blasphemy are also made punishable by statutes in the several States. The cases these statutes take notice of are of a character no one can justify, and their punishment involves no question of religious liberty. The right to use profane and indecent language is recognized by no religious creed, and the practice is reprobated by right-thinking men of every nation and every religious belief. The statutes for the punishment of public profanity require no further justification than the natural impulses of every man who believes in a Supreme Being, and recognizes his right to the reverence of his creatures.

" The laws against the desecration of the Christian Sabbath by labor or sports are not so readily defensible by arguments, the force of which will be felt and admitted by all. It is no hardship to any one to compel him to abstain from public blasphemy or other profanity, and none can complain that his rights of conscience are invaded by this forced respect to a prevailing religious sentiment. But the Jew who is forced to respect the first day of the week, when his conscience requires of him the observance of the seventh also, may plausibly urge that the law discriminates against his religion, and by forcing him to keep a second Sabbath in each week, unjustly, though by indirection, punishes him for his belief.

" The laws which prohibit ordinary employments on Sunday are to be defended, either on the same grounds which justify the punishment of profanity, or as establishing sanitary regulations, based upon the demonstration of experience that one day's rest in seven is needful to recuperate the exhausted energies of body and mind. If sustained on the first ground, the view must be that such laws only require the proper deference and regard which those not accepting the common belief may justly be required to pay to the public conscience. The Supreme Court of Pennsylvania have preferred to defend such legislation on the second ground rather than the first ; but it appears to us that if the benefit to the individual is alone to be considered, the argument against the law which he may make who has already observed the seventh day of the week, is unanswerable. But on the other ground it is clear that these laws are supportable on authority, notwithstanding the inconvenience which they occasion to those whose religious sentiments do not recognize the sacred character of the first day of the week.

"Whatever deference the constitution or the laws may require to be paid in some cases to the conscientious scruples or religious convictions of the majority, the general policy always is, to avoid with care any compulsion which infringes on the religious scruples of any, however little reason may seem to others to underlie them. Even in the important matter of bearing arms for the public defence, those who cannot in conscience take part are excused, and their proportion of this great and sometimes imperative burden is borne by the rest of the community.

"Some of the State constitutions have also done away with the distinction which existed at the common law regarding the admissibility of testimony in some cases. All religions were recognized by the law to the extent of allowing all persons to be sworn, and to give evidence who believed in a superintending Providence, who rewards and punishes, and that an oath was binding on their conscience. But the want of such belief rendered the person incompetent. Wherever the common law remains unchanged, it must, we suppose, be held no violation of religious liberty to recognize and enforce its distinctions ; but the tendency is to do away with them entirely, or to allow one's unbelief to go to his credibility only, if taken into account at all."

DOCUMENT VIII.

George Bancroft on the Constitutional Guarantee of Religious Liberty.

From his "History of the Formation of the Constitution of the United States of America," New York, 1882, vol. ii., p. 326.

"Vindicating the right of individuality even in religion, and in religion above all, the new nation dared to set the example of accepting in its relations. to God the principle first divinely ordained in Judea. It left the management of temporal things to the temporal power ; but the American Constitution, in harmony with the people of the several States, withheld from the federal government the power to invade the home of reason, the citadel of conscience, the sanctuary of the soul ; and not from indifference, but that the infinite spirit of eternal truth might move in its freedom and purity and power."

To this we add, by permission, a private letter in answer to a question of the author :

"NEWPORT, R. I., August 30, 1887.

"MY DEAR DR. SCHAFF :—I have yours of the 12th. By the Constitution no power is held by Congress except such as shall have been granted to it. Congress therefore from the beginning was as much without the power to make a law respecting the establishment of religion as it is now after the amendment has been passed. The power had not been granted, and therefore did not exist, for Congress has no powers except such as are granted ; but a feeling had got abroad that there should have been a Bill of Rights, and therefore to satisfy the craving, a series of articles were framed in the nature of a Bill of Rights, not because such a declaration was needed, but because the people wished to see certain principles distinctly put forward as a part of the Constitution. The first amendment, so far as it relates to an establishment of religion, was proposed without passion, accepted in the several States without passion, and so found its place as the opening words of the amendments in the quietest manner possible. This, I think, is a full answer to your question.

"I take this occasion to express to you my great regard and hopes for your health and prosperity.

"Yours most truly,   GEO. BANCROFT.

"Rev. Dr. Philip Schaff,
"Lake Mohonk Mountain House,
"Mohonk Lake, Ulster Co., N. Y."

DOCUMENT IX.

Christianity a Part of the Common Law of Pennsylvania— Decision of the Supreme Court of Pennsylvania in the Case of Updegraph v. the Commonwealth, February, 1822.

From the "Pennsylvania Supreme Court Reports," *Serg. & R.,* vol. xi., p. 398, Philadelphia, 1845.

"The opinion of the court was delivered by DUNCAN, J. This was an indictment for blasphemy, founded on an act of assembly, passed in 1700, which enacts that whosoever shall wilfully, premeditatedly, and despitefully blaspheme and speak loosely and *profanely* of Almighty God, Christ Jesus, the Holy Spirit, or the Scriptures of Truth, and is legally convicted thereof, shall forfeit and pay the sum of *ten pounds.*

"It charges the defendant with contriving and intending to scandalize and bring into disrepute, and vilify the Christian religion and the Scriptures of Truth, and that he, in the presence and hearing of several persons, unlawfully, wickedly, and premeditatedly, despitefully, and blasphemously, did say, among other things, in substance as follows : 'That the Holy Scriptures were a mere fable ; that they were a contradiction, and that, although they contained a number of good things, yet they contained a great many lies,' and the indictment concludes, to the great dishonor of Almighty God, to the great scandal of the profession of the Christian religion, to the evil example of all others in like case offending, and against the form of the act of assembly in such case made and provided.

"The jury have found that the defendant did speak words of that substance in the temper and with the intent stated. This verdict excludes every thing like innocence of intention ; it finds a malicious intention in the speaker to vilify the Christian religion and the Scriptures, and this court cannot look beyond the record, nor take any notice of the allegation, that the words were uttered by the defendant, a member of a debating association, which convened weekly for discussion and mutual information, and that the expressions were used in the course of argument on a religious question. That there is an association in which so serious a subject is treated with so much levity, indecency, and scurrility, existing in this city, I am sorry to hear, for it would prove a nursery of vice, a school of preparation to qualify young men for the gallows, and young women for the brothel, and there is not a skeptic of decent manners and good morals who would not consider such debating clubs as a common nuisance and disgrace to the city. From the tenor of the words, it is impossible that they could be spoken seriously and conscientiously in the discussion of a religious or theological topic ; there is nothing of argument in the language ; it was the outpouring of an invective so vulgarly shocking and insulting that the lowest grade of civil authority ought not to be subject to it, but when spoken in a Christian land, and to a Christian audience, the highest offence *contra bonos mores*, and even if Christianity was not part of the law of the land, it is the popular religion of the country, an insult on which would be indictable as directly tending to disturb the public peace. The bold ground is taken, though it has often been explored, and nothing but what is trite can be said upon it,— it is a barren soil, upon which no flower ever blossomed ; the assertion is once more made that Christianity never was received as part of the common law of this Christian land, and it is added, that if it was, it was virtually repealed by the Constitution of the *United States*, as inconsistent with the liberty of the people, the freedom of religious worship, and hostile to the genius and spirit of our government, and, with it, the act against blasphemy ; and if the argument is worth any thing, all the laws which have Christianity for their object— all would be carried away at one fell swoop—the act against cursing and swearing, and breach of the Lord's day ; the act forbidding incestuous marriages, perjury by taking a false oath upon the book, fornication and adultery, *et peccatum illud horribile non nominandum inter christianos ;* for all these are founded on Christianity—for all these are restraints upon civil liberty, according to the argument,—edicts of religious and civic tyranny, 'when enlighted notions of the rights of man were not so universally diffused as at the present day.'

"Another *exception* is taken. However technical it may be, and however heinous the offence, still, if it is not charged as the law requires, the plaintiff in error is entitled to the full benefit of the exception. The objection is, that the words are not said to have been spoken profanely.

"We will first dispose of what is considered the grand objection—*the constitutionality of Christianity*—for in effect that is the *question.*

"*Christianity, general Christianity, is, and always has been, a part of the common law of Pennsylvania ; Christianity*, without the spiritual artillery of *European* countries, for this Christianity was one of the considerations of the royal charter, and the very basis of its great founder, *William Penn ;* not Christianity founded on any particular religious tenets ; not Christianity with an established church, and tithes, and spiritual courts ; but Christianity with liberty of conscience to all men. *William Penn* and Lord *Baltimore* were the first legislators who passed laws in favor of liberty of conscience ; for before that period the principle of liberty of conscience appeared in the laws of no people, the axiom of no government, the institutes of no society, and scarcely in the temper of any man. Even the reformers were as furious against contumacious errors, as they were loud in asserting the liberty of conscience. And to the wilds of America, peopled by a stock cut off by persecution from a Christian society, does Christianity owe true freedom of religious opinion and religious worship.   There is, in this very act of 1700, a precision of definition, and a discrimination so perfect between prosecutions for opinions seriously, temperately, and argumentatively expressed, and despiteful railings, as to command our admiration and reverence for the enlighted framers.   From the time of *Bracton*, Christianity has been received as part of the common law of *England.*   I will not go back to remote periods, but state a series of prominent decisions, in which the doctrine is to be found.   *The King v. Taylor, Ventr.* 93. 3 *Keb.* 507, the defendant was convicted on information for saying, that *Christ Jesus* was a bastard, a whore-master, and religion a cheat.   Lord Chief Baron Hale, the great and the good Lord HALE (no stickler for church establishments) observed, ' that such kind of wicked and blasphemous words were not only an offence against God and religion, but against the laws of the state and government, and therefore punishable ; that to say, religion is a cheat, is to dissolve all those obligations by which civil societies are preserved ; and that Christianity is part of the law of *England,* and therefore to reproach the Christian religion is to speak in subversion of the laws.'   In the case of *The King v. Woolaston,* 2 *Stra.* 884 ; *Fitzg.* 64 ; *Raymond,* 162, the defendant had been convicted of publishing five libels, ridiculing the miracles of Jesus Christ, his life and conversation ; and was moved in arrest of judgment, that this offence was not punishable in the temporal courts, but the court said, they would not suffer it to be debated, ' whether to write against Christianity generally was not an offence of temporal cognizance.'   It was further contended, that it was merely to show that those miracles were not to be taken in a literal but allegorical sense ; and, therefore, the book could not be aimed at Christianity in general, but merely attacking one proof of the divine mission. But the court said, the main design of the book, though professing to establish Christianity upon a true bottom, considers the narrations of scripture as explanative and prophetical, yet that these professions could not be credited, and the rule is *allegatio contra factum non est admittendum.*   In that case the Court laid great stress on the term general, and did not intend to include disputes between learned men on particular and controverted points, and Lord Chief Justice Raymond, *Fitzg.* 66, said, ' I would have it taken notice of, that we do not meddle with the difference of opinion, and that we interfere only where the root of Christianity is struck at.'   The information filed against the celebrated *Wilkes* was for publishing an obscene and infamous libel, tending to vitiate and corrupt the minds of the subjects, and to introduce a total contempt of religion, morality and virtue, to blaspheme Almighty God, to ridicule our Saviour, and the Christian religion.   In the justly admired speech of Lord Mansfield, in a case which made much noise at the time—*Evens V. Chamberlain of London.   Furneaux's Letters to Sir W. Blackstone.   Appx. to Black. Com.* and 2 *Burns'* Eccles. Law, p. 95, Conscience, he observed, is not controllable by human laws, nor amenable to human tribunals ; persecution, or attempts to force conscience, will never produce conviction, and were only calculated to make hypocrites or martyrs.   There never was a single instance from the *Saxon* times down to our own, in which a man was punished for erroneous opinions. For atheism, blasphemy, and reviling the Christian religion, there have been instances of prosecution at the common law ; but bare non-conformity is no sin by the common law, and all pains and penalties for non-conformity to the established rites and modes are repealed by the acts of toleration, and dissenters exempted from ecclesiastical censures. What bloodshed and confusion have been occasioned from the reign of *Henry IV.*, when the first penal statutes were enacted, down to the revolution, by laws made to force conscience. There is certainly nothing more unreasonable, nor inconsistent with the rights of human nature, more contrary to the spirit and precepts of the Christian religion, more iniquitous and unjust, more impolitic, than persecution against natural religion, revealed religion and sound policy. The great, and wise, and learned judge observes, ' The true principles of natural religion are part of the common law ; the essential principles of revealed religion are part of the common law ; so that a person villifying, subverting or ridiculing them may be prosecuted at common law ; but temporal punishments ought not to be inflicted for mere opinions.' Long before this, much suffering, and a mind of strong and liberal cast, had taught this sound doctrine and this Christian precept to *William Penn.* The charter of *Charles II.* recites, that Whereas our trusty and beloved *William Penn*, out of a commendable desire to enlarge our *English* empire, as also to reduce the savages, by gentle and just measures, to the love of civil society, and the Christian religion, hath humbly besought our leave to translate a colony,' etc. The first legislative act in the colony was the recognition of the Christian religion, and establishment of liberty of conscience. Before this, in 1646, Lord *Baltimore* passed a law in *Maryland* in favour of religious freedom, and it is a memorable fact, that of the first legislators, who established religious freedom, one was a Roman Catholic and the other a Friend. It is called the great law, of the body of laws, in the province of *Pennsylvania*, passed at an assembly at *Chester*, the 7th of the 12th month, *December.* After the following preamble and declaration, viz. : ' Whereas ye glory of Almighty God, and ye good of mankind, is ye reason and end of government, and therefore government in itself is a venerable ordinance of God ; and forasmuch as it is principally desired and intended by ye proprietary and governor, and ye freedom of ye province of *Pennsylvania*, and territorys thereunto belonging, to make and establish such laws as shall best preserve true Christians and civil liberty, in opposition to all unchristian, licentious, and unjust practices, whereby God may have his due, *Caesar* his due, and ye people their due, from tyranny and oppression on ye one side, and insolency and licentiousness on ye other, so that ye best and firmest foundation may be laid for ye present and future happiness both of ye governor and people of this province and territorys aforesaid, and their posterity : Be it therefore enacted by *William Penn*, proprietary and governor, by and with ye advice and consent of ye deputys of ye freemen of this province and counties aforesaid in assembly mett, and by ye authority of ye same, that these following chapters and paragraphs shall be the laws of *Pennsylvania* and the territorys thereof.'

" ' Almighty God, being only Lord of conscience, Father of lyghts and spirits, and ye author as well as object of all divine knowledge, faith, and worship, who only can enlighten ye minds, and persuade and convince ye understandings of people in due reverence to his sovereignty over the souls of mankind : It is enacted by the authority aforesaid, yt no person at any time hereafter living in this province, who shall confess and acknowledge one Almighty God to be ye creator, upholder, and ruler of ye world, and that professeth him or herself obliged in conscience to live peaceably and justly under ye civil government, shall in any wise be molested or prejudiced for his or her conscientious persuasion or practice, nor shall he or she at any time be compelled to frequent or maintain any religious worship, plan or ministry, whatever, contrary to his or her mind, but shall freely and fully enjoy his or her Christian liberty in yt respect, without any interruption or reflection ; and if any person shall abuse or deride any other for his or her different persuasion and practice in a matter of religion, such shall be lookt upon as a disturber of ye peace, and be punished accordingly.'   And to the end that looseness, irreligion, and atheism may not creep in under the pretence of conscience, it provides for the observance of the Lord's day, punishes profane cursing and swearing, and further enacts, for the better preventing corrupt communication, ' that whoever shall speak loosely and profanely of Almighty God, Christ Jesus, the Holy Spirit, or Scriptures of Truth, and is thereof legally convicted, shall forfeit and pay 5 pounds, and be imprisoned for five days in the house of correction.'   Thus this wise legislature framed this great body of laws for a Christian country and Christian people.   Infidelity was then rare, and no infidels were among the first colonists.   They fled from religious intolerance, to a country where all were allowed to worship according to their own understanding, and as was justly observed by the learned Chancellor of the associated members of the Bar of *Philadelphia*, in the city of *Philadelphia*, in his address to that body, 22 of *June*, 1822, the number of *Jews* was too inconsiderable to excite alarm, and the believers in *Mahomet* were not likely to intrude.   Every one had the right of adopting for himself whatever opinion appeared to be the most rational, concerning all matters of religious belief ; thus, securing by law this inestimable freedom of conscience, one of the highest privileges, and greatest interests of the human race.   This is the Christianity of the common law, incorporated into the great law of *Pennsylvania*, and thus, it is irrefragably proved, that the laws and institutions of this state are built on the foundation of reverence for Christianity.   Here was complete liberty of conscience, with the exception of disqualification for office of all who did not profess faith in Jesus Christ. This disqualification was not contained in the constitution of 1776 ; the door was open to any believer in a God, and so it continued under our present constitution, with the necessary addition of a belief in a future state of rewards and punishments.   On this the constitution of the *United States* has made no alteration, nor in the great body of the laws which was an incorporation of the common law doctrine of Christianity, as suited to the condition of the colony, and without which no free government can long exist.   Under the constitution, penalties against cursing and swearing have been exacted.   If Christianity was abolished, all false oaths, all tests by oath in the common form by the book, would cease to be indictable as perjury.   The indictment must state the oath to be on the holy Evangelists of Almighty God. The accused on his trial might argue that the book by which he was sworn, so far from being holy writ, was a pack of lies, containing as little truth as *Robinson Crusoe*. And is every jury in the box to decide as a fact whether the Scriptures are of divine origin?

" Let us now see what have been the opinions of our judges and courts. The late Judge Wilson, of the Supreme Court of the *United States*, Professor of Law in the College in *Philadelphia*, was appointed in 1791 unanimously by the House of Representatives of this state to ' revise and digest the laws of this commonwealth, to ascertain and determine how far any *British* statutes extended to it, and to prepare bills containing such alterations and additions as the code of laws, and the principles and forms of the constitution, then lately adopted, might require.' He had just risen from his seat in the convention which formed the Constitution of the *United States*, and of this state ; and it is well known, that for our present form of government we are indebted to his exertions and influence. With his fresh recollection of both constitutions, in his course of Lectures, 3d vol. of his works, 112, he states that profaneness and blasphemy are offences punishable by fine and imprisonment, and that Christianity is part of the common law. It is in vain to object that the law is obsolete ; this is not so ; it has seldom been called into operation, because this, like some other offences, has been rare. It has been retained in our recollection of the laws now in force, made by the direction of the legislature,—and it has not been a dead letter.

" In the Mayor's Court of the city of *Philadelphia*, in 1818, one *Murray* was convicted of a most scandalous blasphemy. He attempted by advertisement to call a meeting of the enemies of persecution ; but this ended in mere vapour ; the good sense of the people frowned upon it, and he was most justly sentenced. An account of the proceedings will be found in the *Franklin Gazette*, of the 21st of *November*, 1818. If the doctrine advanced in the written argument delivered to the court was just, (and it is but justice to the counsel for the plaintiff in error for the court to acknowledge the propriety of his conduct in preferring this course to a declamation in open court), impiety and profanity must reach their acme with impunity, and every debating club might dedicate the club room to the worship of the Goddess of Reason, and adore the Deity in the person of a naked prostitute. The people would not tolerate these flagitious acts, and would themselves punish ; and it is for this, among other reasons, that the law interposes to prevent the disturbance of the public peace. It is sometimes asked with a sneer, Why not leave it to Almighty God to revenge his own cause ? Temporal courts do so leave it. ' Bold and presumptuous would be the man who would attempt to arrest the thunder of heaven from the hand of God, and direct the bolts of vengeance where to fall.' It is not on this principle courts act, but on the dangerous temporal consequences likely to proceed from the removal of religious and moral restraints ; this is the ground of punishment for blasphemous and criminal publications ; and without any view to spiritual correction of the offender.—4 *Bla. C.*, 59 *; Fitz.*, 67 : *Stark, on Libels*, 487.

> " ' Shall each blasphemer quite escape the rod,
> And plead the insult 's not to man but God ? '

" It is not an *auto da fé*, displaying vengeance ; but a law, punishing with great mildness, a gross offence against public decency and public order, tending directly to disturb the peace of the commonwealth.   Chief Justice Swift, in his system of Laws, 2 vol., 825, has some very just reasoning on the subject. He observes :   ' To prohibit the open, public, and explicit denial of the popular religion of a country, is a necessary measure to preserve the tranquillity of a government.   Of this, no person in a Christian country can complain ; for, admitting him to be an infidel, we must acknowledge that no benefit can be derived from the subversion of a religion which enforces the purest morality.' In the Supreme Court of *New York* it was solemnly determined, that Christianity was part of the law of the land, and that to revile the Holy Scriptures was an indictable offence.   The case assumes, says Chief Justice Kent, that we are a Christian people, and the morality of the country is deeply engrafted on Christianity.   Nor are we bound by any expression in the constitution, as some have strangely supposed, not to punish at all, or to punish indiscriminately the like attack upon *Mahomet or the Grand Lama.   The People* v. *Ruggles*, 8 *Johnston*, 290.   This decision was much canvassed in the *New York* Convention, 1821.   Debates, 463.   An article was proposed in the new constitution, declaring that the judiciary should not declare any particular religion the law of the land.   This was lost by a vote of seventy-four to forty-one.   It is a mistake to suppose that this decision was founded on any special provision in the Constitution.   It has long been firmly settled, that blasphemy against the Deity generally, or attack on the Christian religion indirectly, for the purpose of exposing its doctrines to ridicule and contempt, is indictable and punishable as a temporal offence.   The principles and actual decisions are, that the publication, whether written or oral, must be malicious, and designed for that end and purpose ; both the language of indictments, and the guarded expressions of judges show, that it never was a crime at the common law, seriously and conscientiously to discuss theological and religious topics, though in the course of such discussions doubts may have been created and expressed on doctrinal points, and the force of a particular proof of Scripture evidence casually weakened, or the authority of particular important texts disputed ; and persons of a different religion, as Jews, though they must necessarily deny the authenticity of other religions, have never been punished as blasphemers or libellers at common law for so doing.   All men, of conscientious religious feeling, ought to concede outward respect to every mode of religious worship.   Upon the whole, it may not be going too far to infer, from decisions, that no author or printer, who fairly and conscientiously promulgates the opinions with whose truth he is impressed, for the benefit of others, is answerable as a criminal ; that a malicious and mischievous intention is, in such a case, the broad boundary between right and wrong, and that it is to be collected from the offensive levity, scurrilous and opprobrious language, and other circumstances, whether the act of the party was malicious ; and since the law has no means of distinguishing between different degrees of evil tendency, if the matter published contains any such evil tendency, it is a public wrong. An offence against the public peace may consist either of an actual breach of the peace, or doing that which tends to provoke and excite others to do it.

Within the latter description fall all acts and all attempts to produce disorder, by written, printed, or oral communications, for the purpose of generally weakening those religious and moral restraints, without the aid of which mere legislative provisions would prove ineffectual. No society can tolerate a wilful and despiteful attempt to subvert its religion, no more than it would break down its laws—a general, malicious, and deliberate intent to overthrow Christianity, general Christianity. This is the line of indication, where crime commences, and the offence becomes the subject of penal visitation. The species of offence may be classed under the following heads—1. Denying the Being and Providence of God. 2. Contumelious reproaches of Jesus Christ ; profane and malevolent scoffing at the Scriptures, or exposing any part of them to contempt and ridicule. 3. Certain immoralities tending to subvert all religion and morality, which are the foundations of all governments. Without these restraints no free government could long exist. It is liberty run mad, to declaim against the punishment of these offences, or to assert that the punishment is hostile to the spirit and genius of our government. They are far from being true friends to liberty who support this doctrine, and the promulgation of such opinions, and general receipt of them among the people, would be the sure forerunners of anarchy, and finally of despotism. Amidst the concurrent testimony of political and philosophical writers among the Pagans, in the most absolute state of democratic freedom, the sentiments of *Plutarch*, on this subject, are too remarkable to be omitted. After reciting that the first and greatest care of the legislators of *Rome, Athens, Lacedaemon,* and *Greece* in general, was by instituting solemn supplications and forms of oaths, to inspire them with a sense of the favour or displeasure of Heaven, that learned historian declares, that we have met with towns unfortified, illiterate, and without the conveniences of habitations ; but a people wholly without religion, no traveller hath yet seen ; and a city might as well be erected in the air, as a state be made to unite, where no divine worship is attended. Religion he terms the cement of civil union, and the essential support of legislation. No free government now exists in the world, unless where Christianity is acknowledged, and is the religion of the country. So far from Christianity, as the counsel contends, being part of the machinery necessary to despotism, the reverse is the fact. Christianity is part of the common law of this state. It is not proclaimed by the commanding voice of any human superior, but expressed in the calm and mild accents of customary law. Its foundations are broad, and strong, and deep ; they are laid in the authority, the interest, the affections of the people. Waiving all questions of hereafter, it is the purest system of morality, the firmest auxiliary, and only stable support of all human laws. It is impossible to adminster the laws without taking the religion which the defendant in error has scoffed at, that Scripture which he has reviled, as their basis ; to lay aside these is at least to weaken the confidence in human veracity, so essential to the purposes of society, and without which no question of property could be decided, and no criminal brought to justice ; an oath in the common form, on a discredited book, would be a most idle ceremony. This act was not passed, as the counsel supposed, when religious and civil tyranny were at their height ; but on the breaking forth of the sun of religious liberty, by those who had suffered much for conscience' sake, and fled from ecclesiastical oppression. The counsel is greatly mistaken in attributing to the common law the punishment at the stake, and by the faggot. No man ever suffered at common law for any heresy. The writ *de haeretico comburendo*, and all the sufferings which he has stated in such lively colours, and which give such a frightful, though not exaggerated picture, were the enactments of positive laws equally barbarous and impolitic. There is no reason for the counsel's exclamation, Are these things to be revived in this country, where Christianity does not form part of the law of the land ! It does form, as we have seen, a necessary part of our common law ; it inflicts no punishment for a non-belief in its truths ; it is a stranger to fire and to faggots, and this abused statute merely inflicts a mild sentence on him who bids defiance to all public order, disregards all decency, by contumelious reproaches, scoffing at and reviling that which is certainly the religion of the country ; and when the counsel compared this act against blasphemy to the act against witchcraft, and declared this was equally absurd, I do not impute to him that which I know his heart abhors, a scoffing at religion, but to the triteness of the topics. It is but a barren field, and must contain a repetition of that which has been so often refuted. It is not argument. He has likewise fallen into error with respect to the report of the judges of the Supreme Court on the *British* statute *de religiosis*, and of *mortmain*, parts of which are not incorporated, as being inapplicable to the state of the country ; these statutes were made to resist the encroachments of religious bodies, in engrossing great landed estates, and holding them in *mortmain*, but these are adopted, so far as relates to the avoidance of conveyances to the use of bodies corporate, unless sanctioned by the charter declaring void all conveyances to superstitious uses. The present statute is called the statute *de religiosis*, from the initiatory words of the act. It clipped the wings of ecclesiastical monopoly, and avoided conveyances to superstitious uses, but had no more relation to the doctrines of Christ than of *Mahomet ;* the counsel has confounded the name *de religiosis* with the doctrines of Christianity, and drawn a false conclusion ; because the statute *de religiosis* was not applicable to the country, therefore religion itself was not, and because they incorporated only part of the statutes avoiding conveyances to superstitious uses, therefore Christianity was superstition, and is abolished. This argument is founded on misconception, and is a nullity. The plaintiff in error has totally failed to support his grand objection to this indictment, for Christianity is part of the common law. The act against blasphemy is neither obsolete nor virtually repealed, nor is Christianity inconsistent with our free governments or the genius of the people.

"As I understand, this writ of error was taken out with a view to decide the question, whether Christianity was part of the law of the land, and whether it was consistent with our civil institutions. I have considered it a duty to be thus explicit. No preference is given by law to any particular religious persuasion. Protection is given to all by our laws. It is only the malicious reviler of Christianity who is punished. By general Christianity is not intended the doctrine of worship of any particular church or sect ; the law leaves these disputes to theologians ; it is not known as a standard by which to decide political dogmas. The worship of the Jews is under the protection of the law, and all prosecutions against Unitarians have been discontinued in *England*. The statute of *William III.* Ch. 3, with its penalties against Anti-Trinitarians, is repealed, and it never was punishable at common law ; and no partial mode of belief or unbelief were the objects of coercion by the civil magistrate. Whatever doctrines were heretical, were left to the ecclesiastical judges, who had a most arbitrary latitude allowed to them. Freedom from the demon of persecution, and the scourge of established churches was not on the *European*, but on our side of the Atlantic. I do not by this allude to any particular church, for the Puritans in turn became persecutors, when they got the upper hand. By an ordinance of 23d of *August*, 1645, which continued until the restoration, to preach, write or print any thing in derogation, or disapproving of the directory to the established puritanical form of worship, subject the offender, when convicted, to a discretionary fine, not exceeding fifty pounds. Scofill, 98. While our own free constitution secures liberty of conscience and freedom of religious worship to all, it is not necessary to maintain that any man should have the right publicly to vilify the religion of his neighbours and of the country. These two privileges are directly opposed. It is open, public vilification of the religion of the country that is punished, not to force conscience by punishment, but to preserve the peace of the country by an outward respect to the religion of the country, and not as a restraint upon the liberty of conscience ; but licentiousness endangering the public peace, when tending to corrupt society, is considered as a breach of the peace, and punishable by indictment. Every immoral act is not indictable, but when it is destructive of morality generally, it is because it weakens the bonds by which society is held together, and government is nothing more than public order. This was the opinion of the court in the case of *Commonwealth* v. *Sharpless*, 2 *Serg. & Rawle*, 101. It is not now, for the first time, determined in this court, that Christianity is part of the common law of *Pennsylvania*. In the case of the *Guardians of the Poor* v. *Green*, 5 *Binn.*, 55, *Judge Brackenbridge* observed, the church establishment of England has become a part of the common law, but was the common law in this particular, or any part of it, carried with us in our emigration and planting a colony in *Pennsylvania?* Not a particle of it. On the contrary, the getting quit of the ecclesiastical establishment and tyranny was a great cause of the emigration. All things were reduced to a primitive Christianity, and we went into a new State. And Chief *Justice Tilghman* observes, that every country has its own common law ; ours is composed partly of our own usages. When our ancestors emigrated from *England*, they took with them such of the English principles as were convenient for the situation in which they were about to be placed. It required time and experience to ascertain how much of the *English* law would be suitable to this country. The minds of *William Penn* and his followers would have revolted at the idea of an established church. Liberty to all, preference to none ; equal privilege is extended to the mitred Bishop and the unadorned Friend.

" This is the Christianity which is the law of our land, and I do not think it will be an invasion of any man's right of private judgment, or of the most extended privilege of propagating his sentiments with regard to religion, in the manner which he thinks most conclusive. If from a regard to decency and the good order of society, profane swearing, breach of the Sabbath, and blasphemy, are punishable by civil magistrates, these are not punished as sins of offences against God, but crimes injurious to, and having a malignant influence on society ; for it is certain, that by these practices, no one pretends to prove any supposed truths, detect any supposed error, or advance any sentiment whatever."

DOCUMENT X.

Christianity a Part of the Common Law of New York.

Decision in the case of the People *vs.* Ruggles, Aug., 1811.

" New York Supreme Court Reports, by W. Johnson," vol. viii., page 293, Philadelphia. Kent, Ch. J. gives the judgment :

" Why should not the language contained in the indictment be still an offence with us ? There is nothing in our manners or institutions which has prevented the application or the necessity of this part of the common law. We stand equally in need, now as formerly, of all that moral discipline, and of those principles of virtue, which help to bind society together. The people of this state, in common with the people of this country, profess the general doctrines of christianity, as the rule of their faith and practice ; and to scandalize the author of these doctrines is not only, in a religious point of view, extremely impious, but, even in respect to the obligations due to society, is a gross violation of decency and good order. Nothing could be more offensive to the virtuous part of the community, or more injurious to the tender morals of the young, than to declare such profanity lawful. It would go to confound all distinction between things sacred and profane ; for, to use the words of one of the greatest oracles of human wisdom, ' profane scoffing doth by little and little deface the reverence for religion ; ' and who adds, in another place, ' two principal causes have I ever known of atheism—curious controversies and profane scoffing.' (Lord *Bacon's Works*, vol. 2, 291, 503.) Things which corrupt moral sentiment, as obscene actions, prints and writings, and even gross instances of seduction, have upon the same principle been held indictable ; and shall we form an exception in these particulars to the rest of the civilized world ? No government among any of the polished nations of antiquity, and none of the institutions of modern *Europe*, (a single and monitory case excepted), ever hazarded such a bold experiment upon the solidity of the public morals, as to permit with impunity and under the sanction of their tribunals, the general religion of the community to be openly insulted and defamed. The very idea of jurisprudence with the ancient lawgivers and philosophers embraced the religion of the country. *Jurisprudentia est divinarum atque humanarum rerum notitia.* (Dig., b. 1, 10, 2 ; Cic. De Legibus, b. 2, passim.)

" The free, equal, and undisturbed enjoyment of religious opinion, whatever it may be, and free decent discussions on any religious subject, is granted and secured ; but to revile, with malicious and blasphemous contempt, the religion professed by almost the whole community, is an abuse of that right. Nor are we bound, by any expressions in the constitution, as some have strangely supposed, either not to punish at all, or to punish indiscriminately the like attacks upon the religion of *Mahomet* or of the grand *Lama ;* and for this plain reason, that the case assumes that we are a christian people, and the morality of the country is deeply ingrafted upon christianity, and not upon the doctrines or worship of those impostors. Besides, the offence is *crimen malitiæ,* and the imputation of malice could not be inferred from any invectives upon superstitions equally false and unknown. We are not to be restrained from animadversion upon offences against public decency, like those committed by Sir *Charles Sedley,* (1 *Sid.,* 168,) or by one *Rollo,* (*Sayer,* 158,) merely because there may be savage tribes, and perhaps semi-barbarous nations, whose sense of shame would not be affected by what we should consider the most audacious outrages upon decorum. It is sufficient that the common law checks upon words and actions, dangerous to the public welfare, apply to our case, and are suited to the condition of this and every other people whose manners are refined, and whose morals have been elevated and inspired with a more enlarged benevolence by means of the christian religion.

" Though the constitution has discarded religious establishments, it does not forbid judicial cognizance of those offences against religion and morality which have no reference to any such establishment, or to any particular form of government, but are punishable because they strike at the root of moral obligation, and weaken the security of the social ties. The object of the 38th article of the constitution was to ' guard against spiritual oppression and intolerance,' by declaring that ' the free exercise and enjoyment of religious profession and worship, without discrimination or preference, should for ever thereafter be allowed within this state, to all mankind.' This declaration, (noble and magnanimous as it is when duly understood), never meant to withdraw religion in general, and with it the best sanctions of moral and social obligation from all consideration and notice of the law. It will be fully satisfied by a free and universal toleration, without any of the tests, disabilities, or discriminations, incident to a religious establishment. To construe it as breaking down the common law barriers against licentious, wanton, and impious attacks upon christianity itself, would be an enormous perversion of its meaning. The *proviso* guards the article from such dangerous latitude of construction when it declares, that '*the liberty of conscience hereby granted,* shall not be so construed as to excuse acts of licentiousness or justify practices inconsistent with the peace and safety of this state.' The preamble and this *proviso* are a species of commentary upon the meaning of the article, and they sufficiently show that the framers of the constitution intended only to banish test oaths, disabilities and the burdens, and sometimes the oppressions, of church establishments ; and to secure to the people of this state, freedom from coercion, and an equality of right, on the subject of religion. This was no doubt the consummation of their wishes. It was all that reasonable minds could require, and it had long been a favorite object, on both sides of the *Atlantic,* with some of the most enlightened friends to the rights of mankind, whose indignation had been aroused by infringements of the liberty of conscience, and whose zeal was inflamed in the pursuit of its enjoyment. That this was the meaning of the constitution is further confirmed by a paragraph in a preceding article,

which specially provides that ' such parts of the common law as might be construed to establish or maintain any particular denomination of christians, or
their ministers,' were thereby abrogated.

" The legislative exposition of the constitution is conformable to this view of
it. Christianity, in its enlarged sense, as a religion revealed and taught in the
Bible, is not unknown to our law.   *The statute for preventing immorality*
(*Laws*, vol. 1, 224.   R. S. 675, s. 69, et seq.) consecrates the first day of the
week, as holy time, and considers the violation of it as immoral.   This was
only the continuation, in substance, of a law of the colony which declared, that
the profanation of the Lord's day was ' the great scandal of the christian
faith.'   The act *concerning oaths* (*Laws*, vol. 1, p. 405. [2 R. S. 407, *s.* 82,])
recognises the common law mode of administering an oath ' by laying the hand
on and kissing the gospels.'   Surely, then, we are bound to conclude that
wicked and malicious words, writings and actions which go to vilify those
gospels, continue, as at common law, to be an offence against the public
peace and safety.   They are inconsistent with the reverence due to the administration of an oath, and among their other evil consequences, they tend to
lessen, in the public mind, its religious sanction.

" The court are accordingly of opinion that the judgment below must be
affirmed.

                                            " Judgment affirmed."

DOCUMENT XI.

The Constitutionality of Sunday Laws.

Decision of the Supreme Court of New York, February 4, 1861. Lindenmuller *vs.* the People. The opinion was delivered by Judge J. Allen.

From " Reports of Cases in Law and Equity determined in the Supreme
Court of the State of New York. By Oliver L. Barbour, LL.D." Albany,
vol. xxxiii., 1861. Pages 560–578.

" The constitutionality of the law under which Lindenmuller[1] was indicted
and convicted does not depend upon the question whether or not Christianity
is a part of the common law of this State.   Were that the only question in-
volved, it would not be difficult to show that it was so, in a qualified sense—not
to the extent that would authorize a compulsory conformity, in faith and practice, to the creed and formula of worship of any sect or denomination, or even
in those matters of doctrine and worship common to all denominations styling
themselves Christian, but to the extent that entitles the Christian religion and
its ordinances to respect and protection, as the acknowledged religion of the
people.   Individual consciences may not be enforced ; but men of every
opinion and creed may be restrained from acts which interfere with Christian
worship, and which tend to revile religion and bring it into contempt.   The
belief of no man can be constrained, and the proper expression of religious belief is guaranteed to all ; but this right, like every other right, must be exercised with strict regard to the equal rights of others ; and when religious be-

---

[1] Gustav Lindenmuller, of the city of New York, had violated the law against Sunday
theatres.

lief or unbelief leads to acts which interfere with the religious worship, and
rights of conscience of those who represent the religion of the country, as
established, not by law, but by the consent and usage of the community, and
existing before the organization of the government, their acts may be restrained
by legislation, even if they are not indictable at common law.   Christianity is
not the legal relation of the State, as established by law.   If it were, it would
be a civil or political institution, which it is not ; but this is not inconsistent
with the idea that it is in fact, and ever has been, the religion of the people.
This fact is everywhere prominent in all our civil and political history, and
has been, from the first, recognised and acted upon by the people, as well as
by constitutional conventions, by legislatures, and by courts of justice.

"It is not disputed that Christianity is a part of the common law of England ; and in *Rex* v. *Woolston* (*Str.* 834), the Court of King's Bench would
not suffer it to be debated, whether to write against Christianity in general was
not an offence punishable in the temporal courts at common law.   The common law, as it was in force on the 20th day of April, 1777, subject to such
alterations as have been made, from time to time, by the Legislature, and except such parts of it as are repugnant to the Constitution, is, and ever has been,
a part of the law of the State. (*Const. of* 1846, *art.* 1. § 17 ; *Const. of* 1821,
art. 7, § 13 ; *Const. of* 1777, § 25.)   The claim is, that the constitutional
guaranties for the free exercise and enjoyment of religious profession and worship are inconsistent with and repugnant to the recognition of Christianity, as
the religion of the people, entitled to, and within the protection of, the law.
It would be strange, that a people, Christian in doctrine and worship, many
of whom, or whose forefathers, had sought these shores for the privilege of
worshipping God in simplicity and purity of faith, and who regarded religion
as the basis of their civil liberty, and the foundation of their rights, should, in
their zeal to secure to all the freedom of conscience which they valued so highly,
solemnly repudiate and put beyond the pale of the law, the religion which was
dear to them as life, and dethrone the God who, they openly and avowedly
professed to believe, had been their protector and guide as a people.   Unless
they were hypocrites, which will hardly be charged, they would not have
dared, even if their consciences would have suffered them, to do so.   Religious tolerance is entirely consistent with a recognised religion.   Christianity
may be conceded to be the established religion, to the qualified extent
mentioned, while perfect civil and political equality, with freedom of conscience
and religious preference, is secured to individuals of every other creed and profession.   To a very moderate and qualified extent, religious toleration was secured to the people of the colony, by the charter of liberties and privileges,
granted by his royal highness to the inhabitants of New York and its depen-
dencies in 1683 (**2** *R. L. app. No.* **2**), but was more amply provided for in the
Constitution of 1777.   It was then placed substantially upon the same footing
on which it now stands.   The Constitution of 1777, § 38, ordained that the
free exercise and enjoyment of religious profession and worship, without discrimination or preference, should for ever thereafter be allowed, *provided* that
the liberty of conscience thereby guaranteed should not be so construed as to
excuse acts of licentiousness, or justify practices inconsistent with the peace or

safety of the State.   The same provision was incorporated in the Constitution of 1821, art. 7, § 3, and in that of 1846, art. 1, § 3.   The Convention that framed the Constitution of 1777 ratified and approved the Declaration of Independence, and prefixed it to the Constitution as a part of the preamble ; and in that instrument a direct and solemn appeal is made ' to the Supreme Judge of the world,' and a ' firm reliance on the protection of Divine Providence ' for the support of the Declaration is deliberately professed.   The people, in adopting the Constitution of 1821, expressly acknowledged with ' gratitude the grace and beneficence of God,' in permitting them to make choice of their form of government ; and in ratifying the Constitution of 1846, declare themselves ' grateful to Almighty God ' for their freedom.   The first two constitutions of the State, reciting that '' ministers of the gospel are by their profession dedicated to the service of God and the cure of souls, and ought not to be diverted from the great duties of their function,' declared that no ' minister of the gospel or priest of any denomination whatsoever should be eligible to or hold any civil or military office within the State ; ' and each of the constitutions has required an oath of office from all except some of the inferior officers taking office under it.

'' These provisions and recitals very clearly recognise some of the fundamental principles of the Christian religion, and are certainly very far from ignoring God as the supreme Ruler and Judge of the universe, and the Christian religion as the religion of the people, embodying the common faith of the community, with its ministers and ordinances, existing without the aid of, or political connection with, the State, but as intimately connected with a good government, and the only sure basis of sound morals.

' The several constitutional conventions also recognise the Christian religion as the religion of the State, by opening their daily sessions with prayer, by themselves observing the Christian Sabbath, and by excepting that day from the time allowed to the Governor for returning bills to the Legislature.

'' Different denominations of Christians are recognised, but this does not detract from the force of the recognition of God as the only proper object of religious worship, and the Christian religion as the religion of the people, which it was not intended to destroy, but to maintain.   The intent was to prevent the unnatural connection between Church and State, which had proved as corrupting and detrimental to the cause of pure religion as it had been oppressive to the conscience of the individual.   The founders of the government and the framers of our constitutions believed that Christianity would thrive better, that purity in the Church would be promoted, and the interests of religion advanced, by leaving the individual conscience free and untrammelled, precisely in accordance with the ' benevolent principles of rational liberty,' which guarded against ' spiritual oppression and intolerance ; ' and ' wisdom is justified of her children ' in the experiment, which could hardly be said, if blasphemy, Sabbath-breaking, incest, polygamy, and the like, were protected by the Constitution.   They did, therefore, prohibit the establishment of a state religion, with its enabling and disabling statutes, its test oaths and ecclesiastical courts, and all the pains and penalties of non-conformity, which are only snares to the conscience, and every man is left free to worship God according to the dictates of his own conscience, or not to worship him at all, as he pleases. But they did not suppose they had abolished the Sabbath as a day of rest for all, and of Christian worship for those who were disposed to engage in it, or had deprived themselves of the power to protect their God from blasphemy and revilings, or their religious worship from unseemly interruptions. Compulsory worship of God in any form is prohibited, and every man's opinion on matters of religion, as in other matters, is beyond the reach of law. No man can be compelled to perform any act or omit any act as a duty to God ; but this liberty of conscience in matters of faith and practice is entirely consistent with the existence, in fact, of the Christian religion, entitled to and enjoying the protection of the law, as the religion of the people of the State, and as furnishing the best sanctions of moral and social obligations. The public peace and public welfare are greatly dependent upon the protection of the religion of the country, and the preventing or punishing of offences against it, and acts wantonly committed subversive of it. The claim of the defence, carried to its necessary sequence, is that the Bible and religion, with all its ordinances, including the Sabbath, are as effectually abolished as they were in France during the Revolution, and so effectually abolished that duties may not be enforced as duties to the State, because they have been heretofore associated with acts of religious worship, or connected with religious duties. A provision similar to ours is found in the Constitution of Pennsylvania ; and in *Vidal* v. *Girard's Executors* (2 *How.* 127), the question was discussed whether the Christian religion was a part of the common law of that State ; and Justice Story, in giving judgment, at page 198, after referring to the qualifications in the Constitution, says : ' So that we are compelled to admit, that although Christianity be a part of the common law of the State, yet it is so in this qualified sense, that its divine origin and truth are admitted, and therefore it is not to be maliciously and openly reviled and blasphemed against, to the annoyance of believers or the injury of the public.' The same principle was decided by the State Court, in *Updegraph* v. *Commonwealth* (11 *S. & R.* 349). The same is held in Arkansas (*Show* v. *State*, 5 *Eng.* 259). In our own State, in *People* v. *Ruggles* (8 *John.* 291), the Court held that blasphemy against God, and contumelious reproach and profane ridicule of Christ or the Holy Scriptures, were offences punishable at the common law in this State, as public offences. Chief-Justice Kent says, that to revile the religion professed by almost the whole community is an abuse of the right of religious opinion and free discussion, secured by the Constitution, and that the Constitution does not secure the same regard to the religion of Mohammed or of the Grand Lama, as to that of our Saviour, for the plain reason that we are a Christian people, and the morality of the country is deeply engrafted upon Christianity. He says, further, that the Constitution ' will be fully satisfied by a free and universal toleration, without any of the tests, disabilities, or discriminations incident to a religious establishment. To construe it as breaking down the common law barriers against licentious, wanton, and impious attacks upon Christianity itself, would be an enormous perversion of its meaning.'

    '' This decision gives a practical construction to the ' toleration ' clause in the State Constitution, and limits its effect to a prohibition of a church establishment by the State, and of all 'discrimination or preference' among the several sects and denominations in the ' free exercise and enjoyment of religious profession and worship.' It does not, as interpreted by this decision, prohibit the courts or the Legislature from regarding the Christian religion as the religion of the people, as distinguished from the false religions of the world. This judicial interpretation has received the sanction of the constitutional Convention of 1821, and of the people of the State in the ratification of that Constitution, and again in adopting the Constitution of 1846.

" It was conceded in the Convention of 1821 that the court in *People* v. *Ruggles* did decide that the Christian religion was the law of the land, in the sense that it was preferred over all other religions, and entitled to the recognition and protection of the temporal courts by the common law of the State; and the decision was commented on with severity by those who regarded it as a violation of the freedom of conscience and equality among religionists secured by the Constitution. Mr. Root proposed an amendment to obviate that decision, alleged by him to be against the letter and spirit of the Constitution, to the effect that the judiciary should not declare any particular religion to be the law of the land. The decision was vindicated as a just exponent of the Constitution and the relation of the Christian religion to the State; and the amendment was opposed by Chancellor Kent, Daniel D. Tompkins, Col. Young, Mr. Van Buren, Rufus King, and Chief-Justice Spencer, and rejected by a large majority, and the former provision retained, with the judicial construction in *People* v. *Ruggles* fully recognised. (*N. Y. State Conv. of* 1821, 462, 574.) It is true that the gentlemen differed in their views as to the effect and extent of the decision, and as to the legal status of the Christian religion in the State. One class, including Chief-Justice Spencer and Mr. King, regarded Christianity—the Christian religion as distinguished from Mohammedanism, etc.—as a part of the common law adopted by the Constitution; while another class, in which were included Chancellor Kent and Mr. Van Buren, were of the opinion that the decision was right, not because Christianity was established by law, but because Christianity was in fact the religion of the country, the rule of our faith and practice, and the basis of public morals. According to their views, as the recognised religion of the country, ' the duties and injunctions of the Christian religion ' were interwoven with the law of the land, and were part and parcel of the common law, and that ' maliciously to revile it is a public grievance, and as much so as any other public outrage upon common decency and decorum.' (*Per Ch. Kent, in debate, page* 576.) This difference in views is in no sense material, as it leads to no difference in practical results and conclusions. All agreed that the Christian religion was engrafted upon the law, and entitled to protection as the basis of our morals and the strength of our government, but for reasons differing in terms and in words rather than in substance. Within the principle of the decision of *The People* v. *Ruggles,* as thus interpreted and approved and made a part of the fundamental law of the land by the rejection of the proposed amendment, every act done maliciously, tending to bring religion into contempt, may be punished at common law, and the Christian Sabbath, as one of the institutions of that religion, may be protected from desecration by such laws as the Legislature, in their wisdom, may deem necessary to secure to the community the privilege of undisturbed worship, and to the day itself that outward respect and observance which may be deemed essential to the peace and good order of society, and to preserve religion and its ordinances from open reviling and contempt—and this not as a duty to God, but as a duty to society and to the State. Upon this ground the law in question could be sustained, for the Legislature are the sole judges of the acts proper to be prohibited, with a view to the public peace, and as obstructing religious worship, and bringing into contempt the religious institutions of the people.

" But as a civil and political institution, the establishment and regulation of a Sabbath is within the just powers of the civil government. With us, the Sabbath, as a civil institution, is older than the government. The framers of the first Constitution found it in existence ; they recognised it in their acts, and they did not abolish it, or alter it, or lessen its sanctions or the obligations of the people to observe it. But if this had not been so, the civil government might have established it. It is a law of our nature that one day in seven must be observed as a day of relaxation and refreshment, if not for public worship. Experience has shown that the observance of one day in seven as a day of rest ' is of admirable service to a state, considered merely as a civil institution.' (4 *Bl. Com.* 63.) We are so constituted, physically, that the precise portion of time indicated by the decalogue must be observed as a day of rest and relaxation, and nature, in the punishment inflicted for a violation of our physical laws, adds her sanction to the positive law promulgated at Sinai. The stability of government, the welfare of the subject and the interests of society, have made it necessary that the day of rest observed by the people of a nation should be uniform, and that its observance should be to some extent compulsory, not by way of enforcing the conscience of those upon whom the law operates, but by way of protection to those who desire and are entitled to the day. The necessity and value of the Sabbath is acknowledged by those not professing Christianity. In December, 1841, in the French Chamber of Deputies, an Israelite expressed his respect for the institution of the Lord's day, and opposed a change of law which would deprive a class of children of the benefit of it ; and in 1844, the consistory general of the Israelites, at Paris, decided to transfer the Sabbath of the Jews to Sunday. A similar disposition was manifested in Germany. (*Baylee's Hist. of Sab.* 187.) As a civil institution, the selection of the day is at the option of the legislature ; but for a Christian people, it is highly fit and proper that the day observed should be that which is regarded as the Christian Sabbath, and it does not detract from the moral or legal sanction of the law of the State that it conforms to the law of God, as that law is recognised by the great majority of the people. In this State the Sabbath exists as a day of rest by the common law, and without the necessity of legislative action to establish it ; and all that the Legislature attempt to do in the " Sabbath laws " is to regulate its observance. The body of the Constitution recognised Sunday as a day of rest, and an institution to be respected by not counting it as a part of the time allowed to the governor for examining bills submitted for his approval. A contract, the day of the performance of which falls on Sunday, must, in the case of instruments on which days of grace are allowed, be performed on the Saturday preceding, and in all other cases on Monday. (*Salter* v. *Burt*, 20 *Wend.* 205.   *Avery* v. *Stewart*, 2 *Conn. R.* 69.) Compulsory performance on the Sabbath cannot be required, but the law prescribes a substituted day.   Redemption of land, the last day for which falls on Sunday, must be made the day before. (*People* v. *Luther*, 1 *Wend.* 42.)   No judicial act can be performed on the Sabbath, except as allowed by statute, while ministerial acts not prohibited are not illegal. (*Sayles* v. *Smith*, 12 *Wend.* 57.   *Butler* v. *Kelsey*, 15 *John.* 177.   *Field* v. *Park*, 20 *id.* 140.) Work done on a Sunday cannot be recovered for, there being no pretence that the parties keep the last day of the week, and the work not being a work of necessity and charity. (*Watts* v. *Van Ness*, 1 *Hill*, 76.   *Palmer* v. *City of New York*, 2 *Sand.* 318.   *Smith* v. *Wilcox*, 19 *Barb.* 581 ; *S. C.* 25 *id.* 341.)

" The Christian Sabbath is then one of the civil institutions of the State, and to which the business and duties of life are, by the common law, made to conform and adapt themselves.   The same cannot be said of the Jewish Sabbath, or the day observed by the followers of any other religion.   The respect paid to such days, other than that voluntarily paid by those observing them as days of worship, is in obedience to positive law.   There is no ground of complaint in the respect paid to the religious feeling of those who conscientiously observe the seventh rather than the first day of the week, as a day of rest, by the legislation upon that subject, and exempting them from certain public duties and from the service of process on their Sabbath, and excepting them from the operation of certain other statutes regulating the observance of the first day of the week. (1 *R. S.* 675, § 70.   *Laws of* 1847, *ch.* 349.)   It is not an infringement of the right of conscience, or an interference with the free religious worship of others, that sabbatarians are exempted from the service of civil process and protected in the exercise of their religion on their Sabbath.   Still less is it a violation of the rights of conscience of any that the Sabbath of the people, the day set apart by common consent and usage from the first settlement of the land as a day of rest, and recognised by the common law of the State as such, and expressly recognised in the Constitution as an existing institution, should be respected by the law-making power, and provision made to prevent its desecration by interrupting the worship or interfering with the rights of conscience, in any way, of the public as a Christian people.   The existence of the Sabbath day as a civil institution being conceded, as it must be, the right of the Legislature to control and regulate it and its observance is a necessary sequence.   If precedents were necessary to establish the right to legislate upon the subject, they could be cited from the statutes and ordinances of every government really or nominally Christian, and from the earliest period.   In England, as early as the reign of Athelstan, all merchandising on the Lord's day was forbidden under severe penalties ; and from that time very many statutes have been passed in different reigns regulating the keeping of the Sabbath, prohibiting fairs and markets, the sale of goods, assemblies or concourse of the people for any sports and pastimes whatsoever, worldly labor, the opening of a house or room for public entertainment or amusement, the sale of beer, wine, spirits, etc., and other like acts on that day.   There are other acts which are designed to compel attendance at church and religious worship, which would be prohibited by the Constitution of this State as infringements upon the right to the free exercise and enjoyment of religious profession and worship. But the acts referred to do not relate to religious profession or worship, but to the civil obligations and duties of the subject. They have respect to his duties to the state, and not to God, and as such are within the proper limits of legislative power. There have been times in the history of the English government, when the day was greatly profaned, and practices tolerated at court and throughout the realm, on the Sabbath and on other days, which would meet at this time with little public favor either there or here. But these exceptional instances do not detract from the force of the long series of acts of the British parliament, representing in legislation the sentiment of the British nation, as precedents and as a testimony in favor of the necessity and propriety of a legislative regulation of the Sabbath. Our attention is called to the fact that James I. wrote a' Book of Sports,' in which he declared that certain games and pastimes were lawful upon Sunday. The book was published in 1618, and by it he permitted the ' lawful recreations' named, ' after the end of divine service' on Sundays, ' so as the same be had in due and convenient time, without impediment or neglect of divine service.' The permission is thus qualified : ' But withall we doe here account still as prohibited all unlawfull games to be used on Sundayes only, as beare and bull baitings, *interludes* and at all times in the meaner sort of people prohibited, bowling.' (*Baylee's Hist. Sabbath*, 157.) Lindenmuller's theatre would have been prohibited even by King James's Book of Sports.

" In most, if not all the States of the Union, laws have been passed against Sabbath-breaking, and prohibiting the prosecution of secular pursuits upon that day ; and in none of the States, to my knowledge, except in California, have such laws been held by the courts to be repugnant to the free exercise of religious profession and worship, or a violation of the rights of conscience, or an excess or abuse of the legislative power, while in most States the legislation has been upheld by the courts and sustained by well-reasoned and able opinions. (*Updegraph* v. *The Commonwealth*, 11 *S. & R.* 394. *Show* v. *State of Arkansas.* 5 *Eng.* (*Ark.*) 259. *Bloom* v. *Richards*, 2 *Ohio R.* 387. *Warne* v. *Smith*, 8 *Conn. R.* 14. *Johnston* v. *Com.* 10 *Harris*, 102. *State* v. *Ambs*, 20 *Mis.* 214. *Story* v. *Elliot*, 8 *Cowen*, 27.)

" As the Sabbath is older than our State government, was a part of the laws of the colony, and its observance regulated by colonial laws, State legislation upon the subject of its observance was almost coëval with the formation of the State government. If there were any doubt about the meaning of the Constitution securing freedom in religion, the contemporaneous and continued acts of the legislature under it would be very good evidence of the intent and understanding of its framers, and of the people who adopted it as their fundamental law. As early as 1788, travelling, work, labor, and exposing of goods to sale on that day were prohibited. (2 *Greenl.* 89.) In 1789 the sale of spirituous liquors was prohibited (*Andrews*, 467) ; and from that time statutes have been in force to prevent Sabbath desecration, and prohibiting acts upon that day which would be lawful on other days of the week. Early in the history of the State government, the objections taken to the act under consideration were taken before the council of revision, to an act to amend the act entitled, ' An act for suppressing immorality,' which undertook to regulate Sabbath observance, because the provisions as was claimed militated against the Constitution, by giving a preference to one class of Christians and oppressing others ; because it in some manner prescribed the mode of keeping the Sabbath ; and because it was expedient to impose obligations on the conscience of men in matters of opinion. The counsel, consisting of Governor Jay, Chief-Justice Lansing, and Judges Lewis and Benson, overruled the objections and held them not well taken. (*Street's N. Y. Council of Rev.* 422.) I have not access to the California case referred to (*Ex parte Newman*, 9 *Cal.* 502), but with all respect for the court pronouncing the decision, as authority in this State, the opinion of the council of revision thus constituted, and deliberately pronounced should outweigh it. If the court in California rest their decision upon a want of power in the Legislature to compel religious observances, I should not dissent from the position, and the only question would be whether the act did thus trench on the inviolable rights of the citizen. If it merely restrained the people from secular pursuits and from practices which the Legislature deemed hurtful to the morals and good order of society, it would not go beyond the proper limits of legislation. The act complained of here compels no religious observance, and offences against it are punishable not as sins against God, but as injurious to and having a malignant influence on society. It rests upon the same foundation as a multitude of other laws upon our statute-books, such as those against gambling, lotteries, keeping disorderly houses, polygamy, horse-racing, profane cursing and swearing, disturbance of religious meetings, selling of intoxicating liquors on election days within a given distance of the polls, etc. All these and many others do to some extent restrain the citizen and deprive him of some of his natural rights ; but the Legislature has the right to prohibit acts injurious to the public and subversive of the government, or which tend to the destruction of the morals of the people and disturb the peace and good order of society. It is exclusively for the Legislature to determine what acts should be prohibited as dangerous to the community. The laws of every civilized State embrace a long list of offences which are such merely as *mala prohibita*, as distinguished from those which are *mala in se*. If the argument in behalf of the plaintiff in error is sound, I see no way in saving the class of *mala prohibita*. Give every one his natural rights, or what are claimed as natural rights, and the list of civil offences will be confined to those acts which are *mala in se*, and a man may go naked through the streets, establish houses of prostitution *ad libitum*, and keep a faro-bank on every corner. This would be repugnant to every idea of a civilized government. It is the right of the citizen to be protected from offences against decency, and against acts which tend to corrupt the morals, and debase the moral sense of the community. Regarding the Sabbath as a civil institution, well established, it is the right of the citizen that it should be kept and observed in a way not inconsistent with its purpose and the necessity out of which it grew, as a day of rest, rather than as a day of riot and disorder, which would be effectively to overthrow it, and render it a curse rather than a blessing.

" Woodward, J., in *Johnston* v. *Com.* (10 *Harris*, 102) says : ' The right to rear a family with a becoming regard to the institutions of Christianity, and without compelling them to witness the hourly infractions of one of its fundamental laws ; the right to enjoy the peace and good order of society, and the increased securities of property which result from a decent observance of the Sabbath ; the right of the poor to rest from labor without diminution of wages;" the right of beasts to the rest which nature calls for—are real, substantial rights, and as much the subject of governmental protection as any other right of person or property. But it is urged that it is the right of the citizen to regard the Sabbath as a day of recreation and amusement, rather than as a day of rest and religious worship, and that he has a right to act upon that belief and engage in innocent amusements and recreations. This position it is not necessary to gainsay. But who is to judge and decide what amusements and pastimes are innocent, as having no direct or indirect baneful influence upon the community, as not in any way disturbing the peace and quiet of the public, as not unnecessarily interfering with the equally sacred rights of conscience of others? May not the Legislature, following the example of James I., which was cited to us as a precedent, declare what recreations are lawful, and what are not lawful as tending to a breach of the peace or a corruption of the morals of the people? That is not innocent which may operate injuriously upon the morals of the old or young, which tends to interrupt the peaceable and quiet worship of the Sabbath, and which grievously offends the moral sense of the community, and thus tends to a breach of the peace. It may well be that the Legislature, in its wisdom, thought that a theatre was eminently calculated to attract all classes, and the young especially, on a day when they were released from the confinement incident to the duties of the other days of the week, away from the house of worship and other places of proper rest, relaxation and instruction, and bring them under influence not tending to elevate their morals, and to subject them to temptation to other vices entirely inconsistent with the safety of society. The gathering of a crowd on a Sunday at a theatre, with its drinking-saloons, and its usual, if not necessary, facilities for and inducements to licentiousness and other kindred vices, the Legislature might well say was not consistent with the peace, good order and safety of the city. They might well be of the opinion that such a place would be ' a nursery of vice, a school of preparation to qualify young men for the gallows and young women for the brothel.' But whatever the reasons may have been, it was a matter within the legislative discretion and power, and their will must stand as the reason of the law.

"We could not, if we would, review their discretion and sit in judgment upon the expediency of their acts. We cannot declare that innocent which they have adjudged baneful and have prohibited as such. The act in substance declares a Sunday theatre to be a nuisance, and deals with it as such. The Constitution makes provision for this case by providing that the liberty of conscience secured by it ' shall not be so construed as to excuse acts of licentiousness, or justify practices inconsistent with the peace and safety of the State.' The Legislature have declared that Sunday theatres are of this character, and come within the description of acts and practices which are not protected by the Constitution, and they are the sole judges. The act is clearly constitutional, as dealing with and having respect to the Sabbath as a civil and political institution, and not affecting to interfere with religious belief or worship, faith or practice.

" It was conceded upon the argument that the Legislature could entirely suppress theatres and prohibit theatrical exhibitions. This, I think, yields the whole argument, for as the whole includes all its parts and the greater includes the lesser, the power of total suppression includes the power of regulation and partial suppression. If they can determine what circumstances justify a total prohibition, they can determine under what circumstances the exhibitions may be innocuous, and under what circumstances and at what times they may be baneful, so as to justify a prohibition.

" The other points made and argued are of less general importance, as they only affect this particular case, and notwithstanding they were ably and ingeniously argued, I have been unable to appreciate the views taken by the learned counsel for the plaintiff in error.

" The law does not touch private property or impair its value. The possession and use of it, except for a single purpose and upon a given day, and the right to the possession and use, is as absolute to the plaintiff in error as it was the day before the passage of the law. The restraint upon the use of the property is incidental to the exercise of a power vested in the Legislature to legislate for the whole State. The ownership and enjoyment of property cannot be absolute in the sense that incidentally the right may not be controlled or affected by public legislation. Public safety requires that powder-magazines should not be kept in a populous neighborhood ; public health requires that certain trades and manufactures should not be carried on in crowded localities ; public interest requires that certain callings should be exercised by a limited number of persons and at a limited number of places ; and legislative promotion of these objects necessarily qualifies the absolute ownership of property to the extent that it prohibits the use of it in the manner and for the purpose deemed inconsistent with the public good, but that deprives no man of his property or impairs its legal value. The fact that the plaintiff in error leased the property with a view to its occupancy for the purpose of a Sunday theatre does not vary the question. He might have bought it for the same purpose, but that would by no means lessen the power of the Legislature, or give him an indefeasible right to use it for the purpose intended, or to establish or perpetuate a public nuisance. The power of the Legislature cannot thus be crippled or taken from them. As lessee he is *pro hac vice* the owner. He took his lease as every man takes any estate, subject to the right of the Legislature to control the use of it so far as the public safety requires.

" The contract with the performers, if one exists, for their services on the Sabbath, stands upon the same footing, and is also subject to another answer to wit, that the contract for Sabbath work was void without the law of 1860. (*Smith* v. *Wilcox, Watts* v. *Van Ness, Palmer* v. *New York, supra.*) The sovereign power must, in many cases, prescribe the manner of exercising individual rights over property. The general good requires it, and to this extent the natural rights of individuals are surrendered. Every public regulation in a city does in some sense limit and restrict the absolute right of the individual owner of property. But this is not a legal injury. If compensation were wanted, it is found in the protection which the owner derives from the government, and perhaps from some other restraint upon his neighbor in the use of his property. It is not a destruction or an appropriation of the property, and it is not within any constitutional inhibition. (*Vanderbilt* v. *Adams,* 7 *Cowen,* 349. *People* v. *Walbridge,* 6 *id.* 512. *Mayor &c. of New York* v. *Miln,* 11 *Peters,* 102. 3 *Story's Const. Law,* 163.)

"The conviction was right and the judgment must be affirmed.

"The summary of the points established by this decision is as follows:

GUSTAV LINDENMULLER, plaintiff in error, *vs.* THE PEOPLE, defendants in error.

"Every act done maliciously, tending to bring religion into contempt, may be punished at common law; and the Christian Sabbath, as one of the institutions of that religion, may be protected from desecration by such laws as the Legislature, in their wisdom, may deem necessary to secure to the community the privilege of undisturbed worship, and to the day itself that outward respect and observance which may be deemed essential to the peace and good order of society and to preserve religion and its ordinances from open reviling and contempt.

"Upon this ground the 'Act to preserve the public peace and order on the first day of the week, commonly called Sunday,' passed April 17, 1860, prohibiting exhibitions or dramatic performances on Sunday can be sustained; the Legislature being the sole judges of the acts proper to be prohibited, with a view to the public peace, and as obstructing religious worship, and bringing into contempt the religious institutions of the people.

"That act is clearly *constitutional,* as dealing with and having respect to the Sabbath as a civil and political institution, and not affecting to interfere with religious belief or worship, faith or practice.

"In the State of New York the Sabbath exists as a day of rest by the common law, and without the necessity of legislative action to establish it; and all that the Legislature attempt to do in the 'Sabbath laws,' is to regulate its observance."

INDEX.

sites, 340–1; returns to Netherlands, 342 ; advises as to West
India Co., and requests compensation, 343–5 ; last letters to Sweden,
346 ; last memorials and death,
347 ; relatives of, 285, 286, 346,
348 ; bibliography of books of,
349–61; unprinted writings of, 361–
68 ; handwriting, 368.
Utrecht, 204.
Utrecht, Historisch Genootschap te,
Berigt, quoted, 201 ; Kronÿk,
quoted, 166, 167, 174, 272, 280,
304, 312, 327, 331, 366 ; wrongly
assigns document to Usselinx, 224.

Valladolid, decree respecting toll,
178.
Vane, *Sir* Henry, 298.
Velden, Abraham van, 310, 311.
Velke, *Dr.*, 306.
Veluwe, invasion of the, 290, 294,
343.
Venice, 205, 267.
Vermuyden, Cornelius, 346.
Verscheyden Redenen, 260, 261 ; ti-
tle, etc., 363.
Versterre, S. C., printer, 295, 356.
Vertoogh, hoe nootwendich, 185, 222 ;
date of, 186 ; described, 190–193 ;
quoted, 177 ; bibliography of, 350 ;
not in Marquardus, 360.
Vervou Jonkheer Fredrich van,
quoted, 206, 216, 218.
Vespasian ridicules superstition about
comets, 112.
Viborg, Usselinx at, 277, 278 ; title
of memorial, 364.
Vigenère, Blaise de, his scepticism
about effects of comets, 136.
Viglius, 319.
Vignaud, H., 322.
Virginia, 210, 221 ; new views of
early history of, Alexander Brown
on, 22 ; character of materials for
such history, 23 ; part taken by, in
establishing religious liberty, *Hon.*
Wm. W. Henry on, 23 ; religious
toleration proposed by, 411 ; Declaration of Rights, 412 ; Ordinance
of, 501.
Virginia Company, 23, 208.
Virginia Resolutions of 1798 and
1799, disputed points about, 74.
Voght, memorials to, 225, 226 ; titles,
etc., 362.
Voigt, F., quoted, 333.
Voigt, G., quoted, 121.
ondel, J. van den, 236, 239.

Voornaemste pointen, de, etc., 228 ;
title, etc., 362.
Voortganck van de W. I. Co., 170,
185 ; not by Usselinx, 222, 223.
Vosbergen, Caspar van, envoy, 253,
254.
Vossius, Gerard, quoted, 124.
Vries, G. de, Az., quoted, 195, 200.
Vthförligh Förklaring, described,
255–9 ; printed, 264, 265 ; copies
sent out, 267 ; quoted, 167, 168,
227, 233, 234, 235, 250, 266 ; bibliography of, 353, 354. See also
Auszführlicher Bericht.

Waerschouwinge over den Treves,
described, 295–7 ; Usselinx rep-
rimanded for it, 298, 301 ; quoted,
170, 177, 242, 288, 292, 294 ; bibliography of, 355, 356.
Waerschouwinghe van de ghewich-
tighe redenen, not by Usselinx,
184.
Wagenaar, 178.
Waite, *Chief-Justice*, decision of,
against polygamy, 418, 502.
Waldenses in Italy, 495.
Wallenstein, 282, 283, 302, 307, 308,
309 ; message from, causes release
of Usselinx, 293 ; relations to Swe-
den and Netherlands, 293.
Walloons. See Netherlands, Southern.
Warmholtz, C. G., quoted, 247, 349,
352, 354, 358.
Warwick, *earl of*, 329.
Washington on religion and morality,
398 ; quoted, 420, 445, 446.
Washington City, attack on, in 1814,
Gen'l Cullum on, 54.
Wässby, ordinance of, for commercial
company, 244.
Watson *vs.* Jones, cited, 439.
Webster, Daniel, quoted, 439, 441.
Weeden, Wm. B., 89.
Wehmo, 276.
Weiwitzer, M., 271.
Welling, *Pres't* James C., on State-
rights, 72.
Welshuisen, Christian, director of
South Co., 270, 272.
Wenzelburger, K. Th., quoted, 170,
175, 290, 295, 326.
Werth, Roland de, 177.
Wesel, 293.
Wesselinck, Jan, of Staten Island,
348.
West India Company, Dutch, proj-
ect of, 169, 176 ; taken up by
States of Holland, 179 ; their draft

Religion in America
Series II

An Arno Press Collection

Adler, Felix. **Creed and Deed:** A Series of Discourses. New York, 1877.

Alexander, Archibald. **Evidences of the Authenticity, Inspiration, and Canonical Authority of the Holy Scriptures.** Philadelphia, 1836.

Allen, Joseph Henry. **Our Liberal Movement in Theology:** Chiefly as Shown in Recollections of the History of Unitarianism in New England. 3rd edition. Boston, 1892.

American Temperance Society. **Permanent Temperance Documents of the American Temperance Society.** Boston, 1835.

American Tract Society. **The American Tract Society Documents,** 1824-1925. New York, 1972.

Bacon, Leonard. **The Genesis of the New England Churches.** New York, 1874.

Bartlett, S[amuel] C. **Historical Sketches of the Missions of the American Board.** New York, 1972.

Beecher, Lyman. **Lyman Beecher and the Reform of Society:** Four Sermons, 1804-1828. New York, 1972.

[Bishop, Isabella Lucy Bird.] **The Aspects of Religion in the United States of America.** London, 1859.

Bowden, James. **The History of the Society of Friends in America.** London, 1850, 1854. Two volumes in one.

Briggs, Charles Augustus. **Inaugural Address and Defense,** 1891-1893. New York, 1972.

Colwell, Stephen. **The Position of Christianity in the United States,** in Its Relations with Our Political Institutions, and Specially with Reference to Religious Instruction in the Public Schools. Philadelphia, 1854.

Dalcho, Frederick. **An Historical Account of the Protestant Episcopal Church, in South-Carolina,** from the First Settlement of the Province, to the War of the Revolution. Charleston, 1820.

Elliott, Walter. **The Life of Father Hecker.** New York, 1891.

Gibbons, James Cardinal. **A Retrospect of Fifty Years.** Baltimore, 1916. Two volumes in one.

Hammond, L[ily] H[ardy]. **Race and the South:** Two Studies, 1914-1922. New York, 1972.

Hayden, A[mos] S. **Early History of the Disciples in the Western Reserve, Ohio;** With Biographical Sketches of the Principal Agents in their Religious Movement. Cincinnati, 1875.

Hinke, William J., editor. **Life and Letters of the Rev. John Philip Boehm:** Founder of the Reformed Church in Pennsylvania, 1683-1749. Philadelphia, 1916.

Hopkins, Samuel. **A Treatise on the Millennium.** Boston, 1793.

Kallen, Horace M. **Judaism at Bay:** Essays Toward the Adjustment of Judaism to Modernity. New York, 1932.

Kreider, Harry Julius. **Lutheranism in Colonial New York.** New York, 1942.

Loughborough, J. N. **The Great Second Advent Movement:** Its Rise and Progress. Washington, 1905.

M'Clure, David and Elijah Parish. **Memoirs of the Rev. Eleazar Wheelock, D.D.** Newburyport, 1811.

McKinney, Richard I. **Religion in Higher Education Among Negroes.** New Haven, 1945.

Mayhew, Jonathan. **Observations on the Charter and Conduct of the Society for the Propagation of the Gospel in Foreign Parts;** Designed to Shew Their Non-conformity to Each Other. Boston, 1763.

Mott, John R. **The Evangelization of the World in this Generation.** New York, 1900.

Payne, Bishop Daniel A. **Sermons and Addresses,** 1853-1891. New York, 1972.

Phillips, C[harles] H. **The History of the Colored Methodist Episcopal Church in America:** Comprising Its Organization, Subsequent Development, and Present Status. Jackson, Tenn., 1898.

Reverend Elhanan Winchester: Biography and Letters. New York, 1972.

Riggs, Stephen R. **Tah-Koo Wah-Kan; Or, the Gospel Among the Dakotas.** Boston, 1869.

Rogers, Elder John. **The Biography of Eld. Barton Warren Stone, Written by Himself:** With Additions and Reflections. Cincinnati, 1847.

Booth-Tucker, Frederick. **The Salvation Army in America:** Selected Reports, 1899-1903. New York, 1972.

Satolli, Francis Archbishop. **Loyalty to Church and State.** Baltimore, 1895.

Schaff, Philip. **Church and State in the United States** or the American Idea of Religious Liberty and its Practical Effects with Official Documents. New York and London, 1888. (Reprinted from *Papers of the American Historical Association,* Vol. II, No. 4.)

Smith, Horace Wemyss. **Life and Correspondence of the Rev. William Smith, D.D.** Philadelphia, 1879, 1880. Two volumes in one.

Spalding, M[artin] J. **Sketches of the Early Catholic Missions of Kentucky;** From Their Commencement in 1787 to the Jubilee of 1826-7. Louisville, 1844.

Steiner, Bernard C., editor. **Rev. Thomas Bray:** His Life and Selected Works Relating to Maryland. Baltimore, 1901. (Reprinted from *Maryland Historical Society Fund Publication,* No. 37.)

To Win the West: Missionary Viewpoints, 1814-1815. New York, 1972.

Wayland, Francis and H. L. Wayland. **A Memoir of the Life and Labors of Francis Wayland, D.D., LL.D.** New York, 1867. Two volumes in one.

Willard, Frances E. **Woman and Temperance:** Or, the Work and Workers of the Woman's Christian Temperance Union. Hartford, 1883.